Susan Mitchell was born in Adelaide and was educated and lived there for most of her life, before moving to London, Melbourne, Brisbane and now Sydney. She has written ten best-selling books, many of which have been published in the USA, the UK, Germany and Holland. Her passion for writing and reading is matched only by her passion for communicating with the widest possible audience. Apart from being a full-time writer, she is a columnist and freelance journalist, a broadcaster and a public speaker. She has presented radio programs on both the ABC and commercial radio as well as her own television program, *Susan Mitchell: In Conversation*. Previously she was a senior lecturer in Creative Writing at the University of South Australia.

Further information about the author can be found at: www.susanmitchellbookclub.com

SUSAN MITCHELL

ALL THINGS BRIGHT & BEAUTIFUL

MURDER IN THE CITY OF LIGHT

MACMILLAN
Pan Macmillan Australia

Founder of a City by Geoffrey Dutton reproduced by kind permission of Robin Lucas
Choruses from 'The Rock' by T.S. Eliot from *Collected Poems 1909–1962* reproduced
by kind permission of Faber and Faber Ltd
Three Dog Night by Peter Goldsworthy reproduced by kind permission
of the author and Viking, Penguin Group Australia

First published in 2004 in Macmillan by Pan Macmillan Australia Pty Ltd
St Martins Tower, 31 Market Street, Sydney

National Library of Australia
Cataloguing-in-Publication data:

Mitchell, Susan
All things bright and beautiful: murder in the city of light.

ISBN 1 4050 3610 9.

1. Murder – South Australia – Adelaide. 2. Murderers – South Australia – Adelaide.
I. Title. II. Title: Murder in the city of light.

364.15230994231

Set in 13/15.5 pt Granjon by Post Pre-press Group
Printed in Australia by McPherson's Printing Group

For Mary, who believes in me, always

The world turns and the world changes,
But one thing does not change.
In all my years, one thing does not change,
However you disguise it, this thing does not change:
The perpetual struggle of Good and Evil.

T.S. Eliot, Choruses from 'The Rock'

I

THE TRIAL

Monday 14 October 2002

HE WAS SO ORDINARY. Short, stocky, bearded, bespectacled. You would have passed him in the street and never paused, not even to register a brief flicker of interest.

I sat, sardine-crushed in the middle of the media contingent, staring hard at him, trying to discern some trace of individuality, some sign that he was, in fact, anything but ordinary. A glint in the eye, a nervous twitch, an erratic hand movement. These were, of course, signatures of the Hollywood serial killer. I had never seen one in the flesh.

But this very ordinary man was still. Stock-still. I looked for something demonic in his stillness but he was as calm as a pond on a soft summer's evening.

John Bunting, 36, was accused of murdering twelve people. Murders so cold, so calculated, so horrendous that the British press had headlined Adelaide, my home town, 'the murder capital of the world'. Tabloid hype, of course, especially if they had bothered to look at the facts. Adelaide is nowhere near the top of the 'murder cities' in the world, rating only 1.9 murders per 100,000 people per year; it is not even the top-rating murder capital of Australia. And yet, the urban myth persists. When confronted with these statistics, those who propagate and relish this reputation lower their eyes and say knowingly: 'Well, it's more the kind of murders that are committed in Adelaide. It's the bizarre, the sick, the twisted, it's the weirdness of them that sets the city apart.'

It is true that the writer Salman Rushdie, having once visited Adelaide for its celebrated Writers' Week, wrote a piece in the British *Tatler* describing Adelaide as a kind of Amityville, 'an ideal setting for a Stephen King novel or horror film . . . sleepy conservative towns are where those things happen'. The myth-makers, of course, leapt upon every word, embroidering connotations with every subsequent conversation.

What was it he sensed beneath the charm of Adelaide's wide, ordered streets, grand Georgian and Victorian buildings and symmetrical leafy green squares? It is variously known as the Garden City, the City of Churches, the Athens of the South, the jewel in the national crown of the arts and sciences. A city, above all, cultured and civilised. But when Salman Rushdie watched night fall in Adelaide, it was not a soft velvet cloak of harmony that he saw descend on this city.

His were visions of exorcisms, omens, shinings, poltergeists and things that go bump in the night.

Now, nineteen years after his visit, details of the most gruesome, horrific, depraved serial murders in the nation were about to be revealed in the courtroom in which I was sitting. Reluctantly dragging my eyes away from the accused murderers, I looked around me.

The desks, the benches, the wood panelling, the dock, the carpet were various shades of brown, public-service brown, schoolroom brown. The colour of dirt. The barristers were clothed in black, except for their string-coloured horsehair wigs. The judge was a solid block of red.

I stared again at the two accused sitting in the dock on my right.

John Bunting, average white male. No distinguishing features. Charged with twelve counts of murder, and pleading not guilty to all twelve counts.

Next to him, his sidekick, Robert Wagner, 30, obviously younger but potentially more threatening in appearance. Tall, blond, balding, with a strong jawline and dead eyes. He was pleading not guilty to eight counts of murder, having already pleaded guilty to three.

He, too, was still but leaning slightly forward as if waiting to pounce.

On my left in their box sat the jury, eight women and seven men. The men were young, in their twenties and thirties, and mostly dressed in grey with open-necked shirts. The women, in maroon and pink, were also casually dressed, all except one in a cream silk shirt. It was as the law dictates: a jury of their peers.

Perhaps for this reason Justice Brian Martin, the red rock, seated high above the barristers and solicitors in their matching black gowns and horsehair wigs, spoke to the jury as if they were children on their first day at school. His tone was comforting, his manner calm, his expression sympathetic. He turned his body towards them.

'Throughout the trial if there is anything you need or want to ask me, then do not hesitate. You will be asked to process a huge amount of information in a very short time. Do not feel inadequate or not up to the task. If you are feeling a little awkward, that's quite natural. You will need to select a foreperson to chair your discussions at the end of the trial but you may delay that selection until you have all become better acquainted.'

He gave them twenty minutes to retire to the jury room to introduce themselves to each other, while the two counsel representing the accused argued points of law with the judge and the Director of Public Prosecutions, Wendy Abraham, QC.

Lead counsel for John Bunting was Mark Griffin, a slightly built, dark-haired, neat figure. Robert Wagner's lead counsel Stephen Apps, on the other hand, was a large, portly, tousled figure with a strong Aussie accent, booming voice and front-bar manner. When the jury returned, Wendy Abraham stood to address them. She was tall, pencil-thin and her clipped, direct tone matched her dark, cropped hair. She was immaculate. Her long, thin fingers clasped the lectern and under the fluorescent lights her pale skin was almost translucent against the bold red of her lipstick and the fragile wire-rimmed spectacles that helped to hold her wig straight. Her only adornment was a pair of small gold earrings. You could almost smell her deodorant. And her discipline.

'Ladies and gentlemen,' she began:

> On 20th May 1999 when the police opened a vault in a disused bank in Snowtown they were met with the pungent smell of rotting or decomposing meat. What they found inside was shocking.
>
> Barrels containing human remains. Knives, handcuffs and gloves, used in the murder, torture and mutilation of bodies. There were eight bodies in six barrels. In the days following the discovery, a further two bodies were found buried in the backyard of a house in Salisbury North.
>
> The Crown says that each of these deaths was part of a series of murders committed by the accused, John Bunting and Robert Wagner. Some time later two further deaths were linked to these series.
>
> As members of the community, your initial reaction may well have been one of horror. Horror of what was found. Horror that it happened here in our community.
>
> Ladies and gentlemen, you have now been called upon to represent that community, to decide the issues in this trial. You will therefore have to put aside any initial reactions you

felt, you will have to distance yourself, in order to calmly and dispassionately evaluate the evidence that you will hear in this courtroom to determine whether the Crown has proved its case against the accused. The Crown alleges that what the accused, John Bunting and Robert Wagner, did in committing these crimes can only be described as horrific. What you will hear at times will be very unpleasant and distasteful. The description of some of the events will be chilling.

Her reading of the list of the victims' names, their ages and the dates of their murders was in itself a catalogue of horror. So many of the men so young, so many murders, one after the other, building in their intensity and frequency.

CLINTON TREZISE, 22, AUGUST 1992
RAY DAVIES, 26, DECEMBER 1995
SUZANNE ALLEN, 47, NOVEMBER 1996
MICHAEL GARDINER, 19, SEPTEMBER 1997
BARRY LANE, 42, OCTOBER 1997
THOMAS TREVILYAN, 18, NOVEMBER 1997
GAVIN PORTER, 29, APRIL 1998
TROY YOUDE, 21, AUGUST 1998
FRED BROOKS, 18, SEPTEMBER 1998
GARY O'DWYER, 29, OCTOBER 1998
ELIZABETH HAYDON, 37, NOVEMBER 1998
DAVID JOHNSON, 24, MAY 1999

What followed was an unemotional, legalistic presentation of the events, purposely devoid of any of the story's drama, no doubt in order for Abraham not to be accused of in any way sensationalising the facts, in the event of a later legal appeal. Yet, no matter how hard she tried to keep the facts neat and orderly and tell the story of these murders in a voice as flat as the Adelaide plains, the pictures overflowed their neat borders and were already starting to spill their sordid contents into my mind's eye.

Wendy Abraham's job was to present a legal case, mine was to write a feature article on what had popularly become known as 'the bodies in the barrels' case. Apart from being Australia's worst serial killings, with twelve counts of murder, the details were particularly gruesome because the accused murderers had allegedly tortured, dismembered and defleshed many of the bodies, and hidden them in barrels of acid in the disused vault of a bank in a country town north of Adelaide called Snowtown. Adelaide was my home town and had long been the source of jokes about its so-called reputation for bizarre and violent killings. My aim was to look for the truth beneath the hype and the headlines. Was there a hidden underbelly to this city that I and many of its citizens either didn't know about or simply refused to face?

As Abraham spoke, the details of the victims' lives unravelled before the packed court like tired knitting, strands of something that once had shape and meaning.

Throughout the prosecutor's monologue, Bunting continued to stare at her. Stone-faced.

How had he ended up living among these people he was accused of murdering?

My research said that he had stopped in Adelaide on his way to Perth because the car in which he was travelling broke down. But why had he stayed on?

While the prosecutor detailed the evidence concerning finger-prints, I began to write the background story as I understood it so far. Just in my head, you understand.

~

When the car carrying John Bunting among its occupants first arrived in Adelaide in 1984, he had no intention of making this small, provincial city in the south of Australia his home. He had left Brisbane – where he had been born in 1966 in Inala, one of the city's poor southwestern suburbs – with the intention of making a new life in Perth, which was booming with entrepreneurial activity. They had been forced to stop because of car trouble but Bunting's travelling companions knew some people who lived in Elizabeth, a depressed satellite town twenty minutes north of the centre of Adelaide by car, and they stayed there in the caravan park.

When the car was fixed, those on their way to Perth were relieved when Bunting said he was going to stay on in Elizabeth for a bit. They didn't want to put up with any more of his ranting about paedophiles and homosexuals and what he'd do to them if he ever got the chance. He'd never let up all the way from Brisbane and they couldn't bear the thought of listening to his relentless tirade throughout that endless, parched desert road from Adelaide to Perth. The bloke was obsessed, they said. Normally quiet, well-spoken and polite, he changed into a raving madman as soon as he started on his favourite topic of hatred and revenge against 'the dirties', as he called them. Even when they had turned up the car radio, he hadn't stopped. He'd shouted louder and louder, working himself into a frenzy. Then suddenly the anger would dissipate and he'd subside into a long, brooding silence. Until the next rage took hold.

Bunting discovered he enjoyed living in Elizabeth and its nearby suburb of Salisbury. Rents were cheap, very cheap. If you didn't like one house, you could just move to another, there were always plenty available. He found the people he met passive and easygoing, if a bit strange. But he liked it that way. They shut up and listened when he talked. And he liked to hold forth. Especially when the rages took over. Those he talked to agreed with his opinions about the dirties, those disgusting low-life paedophiles. They shouted, 'Yeah, man! Right on, man!', when he told them what he'd like to do to them. Mind you, most of them were whacked on drugs or were a bit slow or mentally ill. Didn't worry him. They had their uses.

~

The two accused men continued to stare, unmoved and unblinking, at the Crown prosecutor as she detailed to the jury her account of the murders. I gazed again at Bunting and Wagner. An odd couple. Very odd. How had they met? The prosecutor had the answer.

> The first category of evidence is association. In December 1991, John Bunting and Robert Wagner met each other. On the day that John Bunting and his wife, [V], moved into their rented house at 203 Waterloo Corner Road, Salisbury North, they met another couple who lived nearby at 1 Bingham Road, Salisbury. Their names were Robert Wagner and Barry Lane and they were in a relationship.

~

Number 203 looked exactly like every other house in the street. They had all been built by the South Australian Housing Trust in the 1950s and 60s as part of a plan to attract British migrants to live and work in the satellite towns of Salisbury and Elizabeth. It was a small, square, cream brick box with a tired lawn in front and a desolate backyard. It suited Bunting and was certainly better than the dump in which he had grown up in the poverty-stricken southwest of Brisbane. He had been doing some labouring work at an iron foundry since the nearby abattoir at Gepps Cross had closed and he'd been laid off from his job as a slaughterman.

He was cleaning his prize possession, a BMW motorbike, when his wife, V*, called out through the kitchen window that someone was banging on the front door.

* Name not given for legal reasons.

'Well, answer it. Can't you see I'm busy?'

V did as she was told, stopping only to take off her apron. She was a small, petite woman with dark lank hair and an expression rather like a confused possum's. When she opened the door she didn't expect to see two men with their arms entwined around each other.

'Hi,' said the older one, who was wearing strange yellow-tinted glasses. 'I'm Barry, sometimes known as Vanessa, and this is my fiancé, Robert. We're your neighbours.'

'Hello,' said V, unsure of what to do next. Knowing what her husband thought of homosexuals, she was reluctant to ask them inside, yet she didn't want to get offside with the neighbours.

Undeterred by her silence, Barry said, 'We just thought we'd pop in to welcome you to the street and warn you about the others. Not that they'll do you any harm but a few of them are on parole and you should always keep your doors locked . . . sticky fingers, if you know what I mean. Isn't that right, Robert?'

Wagner had been standing there, hands on hips and legs apart like he was a security guard. Or a gum tree.

'Yeah,' was all he said.

Unperturbed, Barry twittered on in his camp fashion and V just stood at the door hoping they'd go away. She didn't want John getting into one of his rages.

'What's going on here?' John was at her side and he wasn't smiling.

'This is my husband, John Bunting . . . sorry . . . I forgot . . . I'm his wife, V, and . . .' She spoke so slowly that Barry felt forced to interrupt.

'Hi, John, I'm Barry Lane and this gorgeous hunk is Robert Wagner.'

He held out his hand, which was covered in large rings, but Bunting didn't respond.

11

'They're our neighbours,' was all V could manage to stammer.

'Are they, now? Well, you'd better make them a cup of tea.'

V could not believe what she'd heard but immediately took off down the passage to put the kettle on.

After several cups of tea the visitors finally left. Barry had dominated the conversation by describing everyone in the street and giving a potted life history of all their 'closest' friends. V was puzzled.

'John?'

'Yes.'

'I thought you hated fags, as you call them.'

'I do,' he mumbled from behind the paper he was reading.

'Then I don't understand why you . . .'

'Yeah, well, there are lots of things you don't understand, dummy, so let's drop it, eh?'

V, now silent, continued to wash up the cups and saucers. Her bottom lip, which protruded over her prominent front teeth, made her appear sulky even when she wasn't.

Bunting stood up suddenly, knocking over his chair, and slammed the screen door on his way out. V put down her dish cloth, picked up the chair, tucked it under the table and returned to the sink.

~

Barry Lane continued to call around. He was a transvestite and convicted paedophile, and was very happy to talk to Bunting about his life because Bunting seemed interested and Barry just loved to talk. Wagner didn't talk much at first but soon he began to visit on his own with his huge Doberman called Adolf, just to see Bunting.

One night when V had gone to bed early, as was her habit, and it was just the two of them sitting silently in the kitchen

drinking coffee, Wagner suddenly blurted out his troubled history to Bunting. He had been sexually abused when he was
eight, become suicidal, dropped out of school, and been picked
up by Lane when he was fourteen and moved interstate with
him, returning only when he was eighteen. All the time he was
talking he stared fixedly at the pattern in the green Laminex on
the kitchen table. When he finally finished, he looked up to
check Bunting's face. It was grim. Wagner continued to stare at
the green Laminex. After what seemed an interminable silence,
Bunting spoke.

'What he did to you when you were only a kid, that rock
spider, he should pay for. Fucking paedophiles should all be
strung up. Made to suffer for what they've done. Look at you.
Look at what happened to you. Totally fucked you up. How
many years of your life have you wasted? Lane's no better. He
just used you. Picked you up off the street and used you for his
own ends. Fucking faggot, fairy, dirty ass, donut. He just fucked
you and fucked you up. Deserves to be punished for what he's
done to you. Punished in a way he'll never forget. Never. Never.
Never.' He was shouting.

Wagner had tears in his eyes, tears for his sorry, wasted,
fucked-up life.

Bunting continued to shout about how much he hated paedophiles and, as his voice became louder and louder, he became
more and more angry. He thumped the table so hard a glass
jumped off and smashed on the floor. When Wagner rose to pick
up the pieces, Bunting growled at him, 'Leave it, she'll clean it
up,' and just went on ranting and raving until his face was bright
red and little globs of spit were forming at the corners of his
mouth.

'Don't you worry, we'll get 'em,' he kept saying. 'And when
we do, they'll never touch another kid again.'

He said he had ways of dealing with rock spiders.

'I've already bashed more than a few, you know,' he said, fixing his eyes on Wagner, gauging his reaction.

Wagner heard himself snarling like Adolf, his dog. Words failed him. But he never took his eyes off Bunting.

'They always think they can get away with it. Well, I'm going to give them something they'll never forget. You watch me. I'll fix them. Well and truly. Forever.'

A few months later, after more of these late-night sessions and Bunting's repeated soliloquies of hatred and revenge, he took Wagner into his spare room, where he had designed a special 'spider wall'. He showed him the yellow Post-it notes with names on them stuck to the wall and connected by strands of pink and blue wool to map the links between the various people named, all of whom Bunting claimed were paedophiles or homosexuals. Wagner noticed that the name in the middle of the web was Barry Lane's. Clearly, Lane had been very useful to Bunting in supplying names and information because all the people he had mentioned were there, too. Wagner felt a strange thrill of excitement when Bunting pointed to the names and told him he was going to get them all. He made no distinction between paedophiles and homosexuals; they all deserved to be punished.

From then on, every time they were alone Bunting took Wagner into the spare room and they stood side by side in front of the spider wall, like thieves before a master plan. He instructed Wagner in his plans to rid the world of the dirties. When he talked about them he always became very agitated: his cheeks flushed crimson, his eyes bulged white and those little specks of saliva left the corner of his mouth and landed on the yellow Post-it notes. Wagner was drawn to Bunting's anger like a bee to pollen. His words were sweet and he sucked them deep inside himself. Bunting made him feel powerful, made him feel like a man. He told Bunting he had decided that he, too, wanted to take revenge. He wanted to be at his side. Always.

14

Bunting smiled at him. The smile burned Wagner's cheeks, he basked in it like bright sunshine.

Even though Barry Lane complained about the amount of time he was spending around at Bunting's, Wagner didn't care. Lane could continue to whine. For the first time since he had been abused Wagner felt alive, fully alive. He and Bunting spent hours together going over the spider wall, orchestrating exactly what they would do when they got the chance.

Bunting's skills as a slaughterman meant he could describe in great detail to Wagner exactly how he had carved up the animals and stripped the flesh from their bones.

Wagner became very excited when Bunting told him how easy it was and that he could teach him to do it. Bunting was Wagner's hero and he became his faithful follower, even though he continued to live with Lane.

~

In August 1992 when V and Bunting were visiting Wagner and Lane's house at about four o'clock in the afternoon, Bunting suddenly ordered her to stay there and look after the cats. Barry Lane locked her in the house, took the keys and the three of them didn't come back until after it was dark. She was scared but knew better than to quiz her husband about it. A few weeks later Lane arrived at her house, visibly upset. Pacing backwards and forwards across the grey linoleum on the kitchen floor, he kept repeating that he had to tell her what had happened that night. He said it was driving him crazy.

'I'm so upset about it, I can't sleep. I can't eat. Look at how much weight I've lost. I can even get into those old dresses that I used to wear ten years ago – that's the only good thing about it. You must promise not to tell John I've told you. God knows what he'd do to me. Promise. Promise. You must promise and hope to die.'

V promised and spat on her hand to seal the oath, which seemed to calm Lane. He finally sat down at the table.

'Well, when we left – ooh, I can hardly bear to think about it, but I have to tell you because I swear it's driving me insane, feel my heart, feel how fast it's beating.'

V solemnly put her hand on his chest and nodded. As if reassured, he took another deep breath and continued.

'Well, John took us back to your house and there, cross my heart and hope to die if I'm not telling you the truth . . . there, lying in the middle of the lounge room was a dead body. John said that he'd hit him in the head with a shovel and that he needed our help to dispose of the body. Well, I nearly died myself right there in your lounge room.'

'He did it here, in our lounge room?' V was intellectually slow but this was difficult for anyone to comprehend immediately.

She went straight into the lounge room to check the carpet. She scratched at it, she even got down on her knees and sniffed it. Lane followed her, babbling now, with all the details.

'It was here, just by the lounge he was lying, all twisted up and pale, it was so horrible. Ugh. I can't bear to think about it but it haunts me.'

'There's no stains or nothing,' said V, bending down again to get a closer look.

'I don't remember any blood but I could have blocked it out. We picked him up – Robert's so strong, as you know – and carried him to the car and drove to somewhere in Lower Light and we dug a hole, not very deep because the ground was hard like clay but we dug and dug and my arms were aching and then Robert, whose muscles are like steel, well, he took over and then he put the body in and we filled it up and came home. There, I've told you.'

He covered his eyes with his hands.

'Who was it?'

'What?'

'You haven't told me who the dead body was.'

'A friend of mine – an ex-lover, actually.'

'What's his name, Barry? I want to know his name.'

'Clinton Trezise.'

V gasped. And began to wring her child-like hands.

'Oh no. Oh no. Not poor little Clinton. He was so sweet. He used to wear such pretty bright clothes. John called him "Happy Pants". He wouldn't have harmed a flea.'

'But you mustn't tell John I've told you. Promise me. Or he'll be after me next.'

V looked at her watch with great concentration and then pointed at it.

'He'll be home soon. He'll be home for his tea. You'd better go before he catches you here. Go now, Barry.'

Lane grabbed his things and raced for the back door calling out, 'Don't forget your promise,' before he disappeared.

That night in bed, V repeated to Bunting what Lane had told her. Bunting said it was rubbish and ordered her to turn over and go to sleep. She knew Barry made things up but somehow this time she didn't think he was lying. Besides, she hadn't seen Clinton for a long time and he often popped by. Sometimes he even brought her a casserole he had made.

A week later, when he was in a good mood, she asked Bunting about it again. He smiled. A broad, beaming smile while rocking back and forth on his heels and saying: 'I got rid of that dirty and we buried him at Lower Light. Last time he'll wear those happy pants.' Then he laughed. Harsh, scornful. In a second his mood changed and he said darkly, 'Lane has a big mouth and he'd better keep it shut or else.' And then he wheeled on V, gripping her tiny wrist hard in his slaughterman's hands. She winced at the cold vice of his fingers.

'You tell no-one, understand, dummy?'

V nodded.

'Or you know what will happen to you, don't you?'

She nodded again, fiercely.

'Say it.'

She stared at him.

'Say it, stupid.'

'I promise never to say nothing.'

'Don't you forget it.'

And slowly, he loosened his hands, never taking his eyes off hers.

～

The prosecutor told the jury that Clinton Trezise's body was not found until two years after his death, buried in a shallow grave in Lower Light, north of Adelaide. Trezise had no family or close friends. Or, at least, no-one had noticed his disappearance. As she proceeded to explain how the police had collected and compiled the evidence and what the term DNA actually meant, I relaxed back in my seat on the media bench, unaware until then that during the initial brief detailing of the twelve murders I had been leaning forward, my hands clenched into tight fists. My head was reeling. So many young men, lost and displaced, mentally ill, sexually disturbed, constantly moving from place to place, existing on welfare benefits.

The women, all middle-aged and unattractive, mentally slow or mentally ill, all believed that Bunting was interested in them.

The sad and the mad.

And Bunting was the bad.

He had entered their lives, pretending friendship, had even lived with some of them, using them for information for his spider wall. Then, enlisting first Robert Wagner and later young James Vlassakis, the teenage son of his lover, Elizabeth Harvey, as fellow vigilantes, he had systematically murdered them. The victims were human fodder, useful only to feed his hatred, fuel his obsession with punishment and revenge and to reward him with their few possessions and paltry welfare payments.

But how could twelve murders happen over eight years with nobody knowing and nobody asking any questions?

The judge interrupted the flow of the prosecutor's address.

'Perhaps this is a good time to break for lunch.'

Lunch. Forget lunch, I needed air. Big gulps of fresh, clean air.

From outside, the court building looked handsome and solid with its sandstone slabs and terracotta cupola. I put my sunglasses on to shield my eyes from the glare of the harsh midday light. Victoria Square was the square within the planned square that defined the city. Queen Victoria's bronze statue stood dominant, overlooking the green lawns and tumbling red and white flowerbeds. Down King William Street on either side stood the matching nineteenth-century Victorian stone edifices of the post office and the town hall. It seemed that every year, with monotonous regularity, new plans for Victoria Square were proposed and then left to lapse. From its earliest beginnings this was a meticulously planned city and its citizens still believe that one can, in fact, plan for the perfect society. Or, at least, the perfect square.

There was some kind of car rally going on right outside the Hilton next to the law courts; a large, overhanging banner said, 'Classic Adelaide'. Classic, indeed.

I turned left into the arcade that led to the Central Market, where I knew I could get a good strong coffee, or two, at Lucia's. I loved this market and its raw natural energy. In one sweeping glance I took in the men carting boxes of shining apples, the spruikers calling out their bargains, the waxy moons of cheeses, the endless snakes of sausages and hanging meats, whole stalls devoted to mushrooms or chickens, the ever-present earthiness of roasted peanuts, and the wonderful mix of shoppers with their little trolleys stuffing all the fabulous produce into them, weaving and wheeling along the aisles. It was a place that made me want to smell and taste and touch, and hum, 'All things bright and beautiful'.

It had been a childhood ritual that every Friday night my parents, Mitch and Jean, would take me to this market. While they were buying their fresh fruit and vegetables they would often leave me with the Salvation Army Band, which was always belting out rousing Christian tunes on the street in front of the entrance. I was given a tambourine so I could join in and I hit that tambourine like one possessed. In between the brackets of music I would take the collection plate around to the standing crowd, calling them all 'brother' and 'sister', imitating the 'Salvos', as my dad called them. He respected them because, he said, they had been kind when he'd been a soldier in the front lines of Tobruk in the Second World War.

When my parents returned to pick me up, my cheeks flushed with tambourine passion, they always had a big bag of freshly roasted peanuts from Charlesworth's. Yes, the stall was still there and I breathed in the warm, earthy smell of the peanuts. They smelled of innocence.

But it was the imagined stench of rotting flesh that overtook me. I had been taken on a journey to Hades. I had seen a vision of myself standing on an old boat in a dark and terrifying place, eerily silent, except for the thud of twelve decomposed bodies as they banged against the side of the hull.

'Susan, what on earth are you doing here?'

It was Peter Goldsworthy, the writer and doctor, one of my former regular lunching companions along with the editor of the *Adelaide Review*, Christopher Pearson. The *Adelaide Review*, a monthly giveaway, while the product of Christopher's wide-ranging and eccentric interests, was an accurate reflection of how Adelaide liked to see itself and, to some extent, how it still was. It was a journal of politics, social discussion, intellectual ideas and advice on the best places to eat, drink and lead the good life. Adelaide was always a great place to lunch in the grand tradition. The best food and wine and delicious conversation, all taken at leisure, had been our weekly ritual.

'I'm doing a feature on the Snowtown murder trial.'

His face stiffened. 'Nasty business, that.'

'Nastier than you'd ever believe.'

Not wanting to pursue the topic, brisk as always, he said, 'How long are you here? Will you have time for lunch or dinner?'

This was the perennial Adelaide question, passed down from the earliest days of settlement. In a civilised city of easy pace and grace, there is always time to wine and dine. Thank God some things never change.

'Probably not this week but I'll have to come back for further research and I'll give you a ring then. How's Christopher?'

'He's adjusting. You know he sold the *Adelaide Review*?'

'Yes, I spoke to him on the phone recently.'

'Did you? That's good. I'm glad you're speaking again.'

'Well, in spite of our different political beliefs, we have been friends for over twenty years. I think he never forgave me for moving to Sydney.'

In Adelaide the secret code for not wishing to speak about something is to ignore it. He jumped in, 'You know he's moved into a terrace next to me and Lisa in the city – look, I've got to go because I'm due at the surgery but give me a ring if you can.'

Lucia's had not changed. The same unpretentious tables and chairs, scribbled menu, endless bowls of steaming home-cooked pasta. Choosing a secluded corner table – I wasn't much in the mood for bright homecoming chat – I settled for a creamy double-strength cappuccino. Looking down into its froth I wished I could jump into it, like it was a spa bath. Just lie there, letting its warm bubbles surge over me.

～

Back in the courtroom, the woman guiding the boat down the River of Hell, Wendy Abraham, QC, was ready to continue. Everyone had resumed their assigned seats for the journey. The judge, the jury, the barristers, the media, the court sheriffs, the prison guards and the two prisoners in the dock. We were all players in this drama. Outside, we knew, the sun was beating down out of a clear, enamelled blue sky onto the hot plain, outlining the green leafy squares with their ordered rows of spring blooms. The good folk of Adelaide were bustling about their shopping and their business, oblivious to the dark and murky subterranean sewer into which we were being sucked.

'Ladies and gentlemen,' intoned the Crown prosecutor, 'to take up where we left off . . . at the time of their murder, five of the victims were living with either John Bunting, Robert Wagner, Mark Haydon or James Vlassakis. Four of the victims were related to one of the accused. Their lives were all intertwined.

'Ray Davies, the next to be murdered, was living in a caravan in the backyard of Suzanne Allen.'

~

It was Boxing Day, 1995. The weather was sultry, with a gritty north wind swirling discarded Christmas wrapping paper around the backyard. Ray Davies watched it from the small window in his caravan. Christmas presents for her grand-children. How long was it since someone had given him a present?

Yesterday had been just another hot, miserable day. He'd spent it cooped up in the airless caravan, picking at some of the food he'd bought just in case someone had called in to wish him a happy Christmas. Most of the food was still on the table where he had left it. The small block of cheese was sweating and cracking.

A block away, inside Bunting's house, Wagner and Bunting were sharing some takeaway fried chicken. Bunting had tired of his wife, V, and was now living in the same house he'd been in previously, with a neighbour, Elizabeth Harvey, a disturbed and dependent woman who had been in and out of Glenside, the psychiatric hospital in Adelaide. Also living in the house were her sexually abused teenage son, James Vlassakis, and his two brothers, who looked up to Bunting as some kind of saviour in their lives. He had promised to care for them, to protect them from a marauding paedophile neighbour, who had previously sexually abused the boys. They felt safe with Bunting in the house and he fed on their attention and their adulation.

Bunting and Wagner were discussing the possibility of joining the local branch of the neo-Nazi group National Action. Wagner was keen but wouldn't do it without Bunting. In fact, he wouldn't cross the road without Bunting's approval. Bunting, however, wanted to follow his own agenda, not that of a group.

Suzanne Allen, a neighbour, suddenly appeared at their back door. She was breathing heavily as if she'd been running. Silly, fat cow, Bunting called her behind her back.

'What's up?' asked Bunting.

She'd started writing him love letters and while he didn't ever do anything to dissuade her, he never encouraged her either. She repulsed him. He and Wagner used to read the letters aloud and nearly piss themselves laughing, but Bunting told Wagner she could be useful.

Wiping his fingers slowly and fastidiously onto the paper serviette and without getting up, he said, 'Spit it out.'

'Bastard Ray's been touching kids. Daughter and I are going to the cops to report him. Filthy bastard.' She was breathless, panicky. Her eyes darted around the room.

'Where is he now?' asked Bunting, head up, body alert.

'In that bloody caravan of his. You do someone a favour and

23

this is how he repays you. Rubbing himself against kids.' She was teetering on the edge of tears, unsure of whether this would take her a step closer to Bunting.

'You go to the cops. We'll see you later.'

'Right.'

She would do whatever Bunting told her, he was her idea of a man. So strong, so masterful. Perhaps tonight she would have a chance to thank him.

As soon as he heard the back gate slam Bunting jumped up from his chair, his eyes blazing, and turned to Wagner.

'Forget the Nazis, this is our chance. Get your car keys. We're going to take this dirty for a little ride.' Wagner felt a current of excitement so strong it was as if someone had plugged him into a live socket.

~

On Bunting's orders he dragged Ray Davies out of the caravan by his hair.

'Shove him in the boot.'

Wagner did as he was ordered. Davies crouched in the boot of the old Torana, his hands up in front of his face as protection. He was whimpering.

Bunting started bashing him on the head, the whole time keeping up a running commentary about filthy, dirty pae-dophiles. Wagner stood by his side, his fists clenched, poised for a signal to join in.

'So you rubbed yourself up against a kid, did you? Couldn't help yourself. Just had to hit on a kid. Bad boy. Dirty boy. And you know what happens to bad, dirty boys?'

He looked at Wagner and smiled. That smile was all Wagner needed. He smashed his fist as hard as he could down onto the side of Davies' head. Again and again he bashed him in a kind of blind frenzy until Davies slumped unconscious back into the boot. Bunting slammed it shut and they drove to a nearby town called Bakara. Being the day after Christmas, there weren't many cars on the road and the wind was belching its hot breath through the open windows.

'Hungry?' Bunting shouted at Wagner. 'Let's leave him in the boot and get something to eat.' Bunting pulled off the road into a nearby service station and, while they ate their hamburgers, Bunting talked. He was hyped. Wagner listened. If he'd been a dog, his tail would have been thumping on the floor.

'You've got to have a plan. You've got to know what you're doing. You've got to know why you're doing it. Otherwise, it can get away from you. Out of control. It's all about planning. Detailed planning. Sifting through all the facts. Knowing how to cover your arse. Knowing how to react to the unexpected. I know what I'm doing here, so don't ask any questions, just do as I say. This is it. This is your chance. You up to it? Don't fuck me around.'

'Just let me at him.'

Wagner's fist was clenched, his knuckles stretched white. His grin was all teeth and saliva.

When they had finished eating and Bunting had meticulously wiped his hands clean, they drove back to 203 Waterloo Corner Road, where Wagner dragged Davies' limp form out of the car and shoved him in the bathtub. He was conscious but not making any noise, his eyes bulging and wide with shock. Bunting had taken a steel pole out of the car and was using it to whip Davies in the balls. The more they swelled up, the more he laughed. He told Wagner to go to the wooden cabinet in the kitchen, to open its leadlight doors and take out the handcuffs, and then go to the spare bedroom and get the jumper leads out of the white cupboard.

When Suzanne Allen and her daughter, Annette, returned from the police station they went straight to the caravan. Davies had disappeared. When he hadn't returned by five o'clock Suzanne put on some bright red lipstick, fluffed up her hair and walked the block to Bunting's house. Wagner and Bunting were sitting in the kitchen, both of them in high spirits, laughing and joking. She had never seen John like this before. They appeared not even to notice she was there.

'Where's Ray?'

'We took him for a little drive to Bakara, didn't we?' Bunting asked Wagner. They both snorted as if it was a huge joke. Suzanne laughed too, and flashed her eyes at Bunting. But he was looking at Robert.

'And then we bashed some sense into him,' said Wagner, his eyes like hot coals, 'bashed him. Like this.' And he clenched his fist and made a downward pounding motion, smashing his fist into the Laminex.

Bunting laughed and copied his action. Trying to match their mood, Suzanne said, 'And then what did you do?'

There was a pause, a beat.

Bunting stopped smiling and said in a low growl, 'Then we pushed him out of the car into the scrub and told him to walk home.'

'That's a long way away. He's probably still walking,' Suzanne giggled, flirtatious and silly.

Bunting said, without looking at her, 'Don't you have to get home?'

She knew it was an order and promptly obeyed. Tonight was clearly not the night for personal declarations of love, she thought to herself as she panted along the footpath.

~

Ray Davies' name was on the spider wall. A strand of pink wool linked him to Barry Lane. On 20 January 1996, his caravan was towed from Suzanne Allen's backyard to Bunting's friend

Mark Haydon's house nearby. It was sold from there and payments were made, in instalments, to 203 Waterloo Corner Road.

In the words of the prosecutor, 'Within four weeks of Ray Davies' disappearance, his property had been taken, his caravan sold and Bunting was being paid for the caravan. Ray Davies' Centrelink benefits were maintained and withdrawals made regularly from his account.'

~

'Knives, handcuffs, a Variac machine, gloves, handcuff keys, sparklers, tape, rope. These were the implements or paraphernalia that the accused used to torture their victims.'

The prosecutor had brought me back to the courtroom with a jolt. I refocused on my notebook.

> Bunting and Wagner enjoyed torturing and murdering their victims. They would laugh, joke, boast and indeed brag about the murders they had committed. James Vlassakis will provide an eyewitness account of the murders of Troy Youde, Fred Brooks, Gary O'Dwyer and David Johnson. Vlassakis's account will include the lead-up to the murder, what was involved in committing the murder, the disposing of the body, the taking of a victim's property, the claiming of Centrelink benefits and the telling of false stories.
>
> It is alleged that with the exception of Suzanne Allen, John Bunting admitted committing each of these murders to James Vlassakis.
>
> In relation to Suzanne Allen, he did, however, make admissions in relation to the mutilation of the body. When Bunting spoke of the murders within this group, it is alleged that Wagner was party to the conversation and joined in by his words or actions. They were frequently spoken of when

Bunting and Wagner were together with Vlassakis.
Bunting and Wagner boasted or bragged how they had
killed particular people and what they had done to them.
On occasions they'd be laughing and joking. In these
conversations they would jump from murder to murder
and sometimes compare how a particular victim reacted or
handled what was being done to them.

In this context, certain words or phrases were used by
Bunting and Wagner, which had a particular meaning. For
example, words such as 'dirty', that was used to describe
a paedophile. They were a dirty. On another level there
were words or phrases that particularly related to the
murders.

For example, if it was said that a person needed to 'go to
the clinic', it meant the person needed to be killed. John
Bunting explained to Vlassakis that this term meant that the
victim had a disease and they needed to go to the clinic to be
made good. Once they were dead, they had been made good.
The term 'smurf', or smurfing, a smurf is a small elf-like
character that was blue in colour. Smurfing referred to killing.
'First you go blue, then you go poo.' That's what the accused
would say. Wagner would say he enjoyed making smurfs, or
smurfing. At times Bunting referred to Wagner as Papa
Smurf.

There's a reference to the term 'slice and dice', which was
when a body was to be cut up or mutilated.

Vlassakis is committed as guilty to four murders, Troy
Youde, Fred Brooks, Gary O'Dwyer and David Johnson.
He has been sentenced to life imprisonment, with a
non-parole period of 26 years. It clearly would have been
higher, but for his guilty pleas and cooperation with the
authorities.

I thought about how Bunting must hate James Vlassakis. If he had killed him along with the others, there would have been no witnesses to any of the murders. Wagner was too far steeped in blood and gore to betray him. Besides, he would never have turned Crown witness against his leader. No wonder Vlassakis was being held in a secret tight-security prison. The Crown's chief witness had to be protected, especially now.

'And so,' continued the prosecutor, 'we come to the details of the third murder. That of Suzanne Allen, who disappeared eleven months after Ray Davies.'

~

Bunting was rearranging some of the Post-it notes on the spider wall when Wagner opened the door and told him that Suzanne Allen was in the kitchen, again, pleading to see him. Bunting liked to see things in their proper order. He hated mess. He was personally meticulous. His nails were scrubbed and clipped short, his teeth flossed, his nasal hair trimmed. He had never smoked, never drank, never took drugs.

'Tell her to piss off. Tell her I'm asleep, tell her anything.'

'She's very insistent. Keeps going on and on about Ray Davies. I think you'd better shut her up. She's the street gossip. Talks to everyone. That big mouth is never closed.'

Bunting sighed, pinned the pink wool hard into the chart, straightened one of the yellow notes and closed the door to the spare room firmly behind him. He didn't want that fat nosey parker getting her beady eyes on it.

Why didn't she just shut up? What was her problem? She hated Ray for what he did to kids. Why did she care what had happened to him? He was a dirty. He was a waste of oxygen. Why did she keep going on about what had happened to him? If she didn't shut that flapping big red ugly slash of a mouth of hers, someone would have to shut it for her.

'What's wrong now?' Terse, impatient.

'John, John, don't speak to me like that.' Wheedling, whining.

'What's that letter in your hand? Not another one of yours, I hope.'

'It's from Centrelink. It's for Ray. Should I ring them and tell them that he disappeared?'

'You'll tell them nothing. Nothing. You understand?'

He took a step closer to her. She held her ground. She liked to feel him up close to her body.

'John, John, you know I hate it when you speak harshly to me. It gets me all upset for the rest of the day.'

She slumped dramatically onto the chair and put her head in her hands. An anguished sob like a tiny earthquake shook her entire body.

His tone softer now, more persuasive: 'I just don't want you to have to worry about it. Let me deal with it. Trust me.'

'I do trust you, John. You know I do. I'd trust you with my life. You know I feel there's something strong between us.'

'Just do as I tell you.'

'I will, John, I will.'

'Now, give me the letter and don't discuss this with anyone. Right?'

'Right. Will I see you tonight?'

'Perhaps. You have to go now because I have to deal with this.'

'See you tonight, then.'

She stepped forward as if to kiss him, but when he stepped back, she blew him a kiss before disappearing out the back door, which slammed after her in the wind.

'Do you reckon she'll keep her mouth shut?' he asked Wagner.

'Na. Can't help herself.'

'Stupid cunt.'

'Stupid, fat-titted cunt.'

'Stupid, fat-titted, big-arsed cunt.'
'Stupid, fat-titted, big-arsed, cow-headed cunt.'

~

Bunting and Wagner pleaded not guilty to the murder of Suzanne Allen, both insisting that when they had arrived at her house, she was already dead from a heart attack. The prosecution did not believe them. They did admit, however, to being guilty of mutilating her body after she was dead. Together they cut off her head, her arms, her legs, her breasts and her genitals. By the time they had finished, her body was almost entirely defleshed. Somewhere in this frenzy of misogyny and butchery, Wagner became so ebullient that he held up the head of Suzanne Allen in both his hands and, thrusting it towards Bunting, said, 'Kiss the puppet.'

After the mutilation, Bunting and Wagner made several visits to Allen's house to go through her property. When they saw a hire-truck parked out the front and two men carrying some of Allen's belongings into it, her neighbours, Marilyn Nelson and Dianne Arthur, decided to knock on the front door. They later reported to the police that the man who answered the door was short and stocky and that behind him they saw a taller man with blondish hair going through Allen's cabinet. They asked to see Allen's brother but the man who answered the door said he didn't know him. Dissatisfied with his response, they went to the police.

On 3 December 1996, two policemen knocked on the front door of Suzanne Allen's house. Again it was Bunting who opened the door and Bunting who did all the talking. After the police had taken their names and seen their identification, he explained that they were helping a friend, Suzanne Allen, move out. He gave the police the phone number of Elizabeth Harvey, James Vlassakis's mother, who could be rung for verification.

After fifteen minutes of questioning, the police left, satisfied with their bona fides. Bunting and Wagner immediately drove Allen's car to Wagner's mother's house, where they stored it for some time.

Bunting contacted Carol Parker, Allen's friend, and explained that Suzanne was 'dressing like a tart' because she was going out with Andy, a guy who was twenty years younger than her, that she owed one thousand dollars for work done on her car and that she was in hiding. In January 1997 when she was reported as a missing person, Bunting rang Missing Persons, identifying himself as Ray Davies, her ex de facto, and told them that he had heard from Allen just before Christmas and that she was living in hiding with Andy in Murray Bridge because she was in trouble with the police.

The police report stated:

> On the 23rd May, '99, police began digging in an area in the backyard of 203 Waterloo Corner Road. About seven centimetres from the surface they were met with concrete. This was removed and the excavation continued. At another 1.37 metres was a garbage bag. Another ten bags were found either next to or underneath each other. The deepest was approximately 1.75 metres from the surface.
>
> One of the bags was opened and what appeared to be human remains were inside. There was a strong odour of decomposition released on the opening of the bag. All of these bags were marked and taken to the Forensic Science Centre. It is alleged in these bags were the remains of Suzanne Allen.
>
> Three days later on the 26th May, '99 the police reattended at 203 Waterloo Corner Road, Salisbury North and continued to dig beneath the area where the bags containing Suzanne Allen had been located. Earthmoving equipment was used. At a depth of approximately 1.9 metres from the surface were

human skeletal remains. The skeleton was unclothed, except for a green parka hood around the skull. It was removed and taken to the Forensic Science Centre. It was that of Ray Davies.

~

Sliced and diced.

First they went blue, then they went poo.

Papa Smurf – Robert Wagner – was now a graduate of the John Bunting Academy of Murder and Mutilation.

~

At 4 pm the judge cleared his throat and said he thought the prosecutor could stop now and continue her opening address tomorrow. Good call, Your Honour. I needed to go back to my hotel, have a stiff drink and reread my notes just to make sure that the pictures swirling around in my head were consistent with the facts.

This was truly the stuff of Hollywood horror movies, not provincial Adelaide. Perhaps Salman Rushdie had been right, after all. Perhaps this was Amityville, with an Aussie veneer of respectability and culture. Perhaps because I had grown up here, I just couldn't sense it as Rushdie seemed to have done.

The judge turned again towards the jury and reminded them that it was inappropriate to attempt to get further information from the Internet, as it is not accountable to anyone for accuracy and there may be assertions of fact that are wrong. He urged them to keep an open mind until they had heard the entire Crown position. I wondered how they were feeling about being members of this jury. This was, after all, only day one. They had months of this, perhaps even a year, ahead of them. I had heard the expression 'stunned mullet' but never known exactly how it felt. Or looked, until I stared at this jury. My face probably portrayed the same expression.

Turning his attention to everyone in the courtroom, the judge paused, as if taking a deep breath. It was an extended pause. The court was as silent and still as the accused in the dock.

'I'm afraid I have just received some extremely distressing news. A senior public servant has been gunned down outside her office in Hindmarsh Square. So be very careful as you leave the building. The Star Force are in the streets and on the lookout for the killer. I urge you to take care.'

We stared at each other in total disbelief . . . I had heard some shocking things in this courtroom today but this was really insane. What kind of city had I come home to? While the local journalists launched themselves into a frenzy of phone calls, I fled, my head down, legs flying across the grey pavements back to my suite at the Medina in time to catch the five o'clock television news.

With a stiff gin and tonic in my hand I stared in further disbelief at the opening item. What I saw on the screen was the now former director of South Australia's Mental Health Services, Margaret Tobin, being wheeled out of her building on an ambulance trolley, only her black-stockinged feet sticking out from under the white cover. For her, today had started out as just another Monday. Hers was a very difficult job. The increasing deinstitutionalisation of the mentally ill had become a nightmare for public servants in her position. The reporter explained that the director had been out to a café for lunch, as was her usual habit, and walked back to her building, taking the lift to her floor. Just as she was stepping out, a man who had been riding next to her stepped out of the lift, gunned her down, stepped back into the lift, pressed the button and disappeared.

I poured myself another stiff drink. I was going nowhere tonight.

Tuesday 15 October 2002

'CLASSIC ADELAIDE', the tourism event involving classic cars, had erected a stage directly in front of the Hilton. There were entrances and exits for the cars to rev up the gangplanks and pause to have their moment of glory while the exuberant emcee proclaimed their attributes over a very loud sound system. On this sunny Adelaide morning as I squeezed my way along the footpath through the crush of people who were admiring the beautiful old cars, I couldn't help thinking about the killer who was still at large. Was he standing nearby, undetected? A murderer with a passion for classic cars? No – far too Agatha Christie. Get a grip, girl.

Inside the doors of the courts' foyer and through the security check I slowly mounted the long, white marble staircase. This marble had been specially transported from Carrara in Italy and matched the marble used for the building of Adelaide's Parliament House. It was a very grand and a very beautiful staircase, once the centrepiece of the Charles Moore Department Store, which had been built on the site in 1912. Only the building's facade and this staircase had survived a terrible fire in 1948. The store was rebuilt but the staircase was dismantled in 1981 to allow for the construction of the present Sir Samuel Way Law Courts, after which it was reassembled within the historic facade of the original building. I knew all this because I read it on the brass plaque that commemorates the opening of the courts on 7 November 1982 by the Lieutenant Governor, the Hon. Sir Condor Laucke, KCMG. We were all standing around, waiting, outside the locked door to the court.

The delayed start gave the media contingent twenty minutes to discuss the rumours that we were being held up because a member of the press had transgressed and broken a suppression order, and that the murder of the director of Mental Health Services had probably been a professional hit. We all had our theories but none of us knew the facts.

The doors to the courtroom finally opened and we took our seats, standing again briefly, as protocol demanded, to acknowledge the judge's entry. The reason we had been kept waiting, the judge explained, was that after yesterday's opening statement a member of the jury had decided that she was unable to continue. He had discharged the juror. Therefore – and here he paused to maximise the impact of what he was about to say – in the light of this loss on only the first day of the trial, he had made the decision to discharge this jury and start with a new one tomorrow. He simply couldn't afford to lose one juror after only one day; it was better to discharge this group and start again.

This meant beginning again from the beginning. Wendy Abraham would have to say it all over again to a new jury.

There was a collective groan, faint but audible. Both the accused remained unblinking and visibly unmoved. Why should they care, they had no plans to go anywhere. For them, it was another day out of jail. Another day when they would be the centre of attention.

I left the courtroom, scowling into the harsh sunlight. A man in a black leather jacket pushed past me. His face had a haunted look. The local paper this morning had stated that the police had no clues as to the executioner of the director of Mental Health Services, apart from the fact that he was a Caucasian male of medium height, in his early twenties. I stared at every male who fitted this description. In Adelaide, still a predominantly WASP city, there were a lot of them. I reminded myself that Bunting, accused of murdering twelve people, looked ordinary. Normal, even. Whatever that means.

I had to force myself to stop focusing on men who looked deranged or wild-eyed or who were covered in tattoos. I told myself to forget every stereotype that had ever lodged in my head. All secrets, not just of murderers, are hidden, or disguised, lurking somewhere in the conscious or unconscious mind.

It seemed some of Adelaide's darkest secrets, however, would never be solved. Like what happened to the Beaumont children. I remembered my parents talking in hushed tones about how shocking it was that three children who had left for a day at the beach had never returned home. 'How could such a thing happen in Adelaide, of all places?' they constantly asked each other, as if repeating this mantra would erase the truth. Every day after that when I left home I was told, 'Take care, remember the Beaumont children.' The fact that I was nineteen years of age at the time seemed to have escaped them.

This is the story anyone living in Adelaide at the time can tell you. We all know it off by heart. It's village folklore.

On the hot and humid morning of 26 January 1966, Jane Beaumont, nine, Arnna, seven, and Grant, four, kissed their mother goodbye, left their nice suburban home and caught the bus just outside their front door to the nearby Glenelg Beach.

When they had failed to return home by late afternoon, the police were alerted. What followed was an Australia-wide search, with the children's photos on the front page of every newspaper in the country. Witnesses came forward to say they had been seen in the company of a tall blond or light-brown-haired young man in blue bathers, both in the park opposite the beach and walking away with him behind the Glenelg Hotel.

For years it seemed possible that another clue would be found to their disappearance. The police even imported an internationally famous Dutch clairvoyant to help them in their search. The cement floor of a warehouse was dug up but not a trace of the children has ever been found. Rumours of their whereabouts persist.

Then, in August 1973, two young girls, eleven and seven, were abducted from a football match they were attending with their parents at the Adelaide Oval. They, too, were never heard of again. Police and the public speculated that the two disappearances were linked but no links were ever found.

In the late 1970s the bodies of seven teenage girls who had all been abducted from the city or the northern suburbs were discovered in scrubland near the small country town of Truro, which is about 80 kilometres north of Adelaide on the way to the lush vineyards of the Barossa Valley. One of the two men responsible, James Miller, was convicted of six of the murders; the other had been killed in a traffic accident two days after the disappearance of the last victim.

The 1980s revealed their own sordid secrets when the bodies of five young men were found. These were known as the Family Murders and all the bodies of the young men who were found were either buried in the foothills or floating in plastic bags in the Port River. They had been sexually assaulted, and mutilated. The convicted killer, Bevan Spencer von Einem – a name that still chills the heart of anyone who was living in Adelaide during that period – was also suspected of being implicated in the disappearance of the Beaumont children but even now remains in jail, denying any involvement. The Beaumont case has to this day never been solved.

This history of the crimes of abduction, torture and murder of young people has no doubt been responsible for Adelaide's reputation as a city of sick and bizarre murders. As one of Adelaide's celebrated writers, Barbara Hanrahan, had reminded everyone, 'Even when the animals in the zoo were attacked [in the 1980s], it was the baby animals they slaughtered. Adelaide,' she said, 'is weird.'

When you live in a small city, everyone remembers everything. I was starting to spook myself.

Wednesday 16 October 2002   Groundhog Day

SAME JUDGE. Same lawyers. Same counsel for the prosecution. Same counsels for the defence. Same media contingent sitting in the same seats.

Different jury.

Again Wendy Abraham, QC rose to address them, her voice betraying no emotion, her presentation, as before, purposefully matter-of-fact and non-inflammatory. She started from the beginning. I tried to look on the positive side – at least I would be able to check my notes from Monday. I'll skip what you have already heard.

'And now we come to the fourth victim, Michael Gardiner, who disappeared in September 1997.'

During this year Robert Wagner had moved in with a woman and her children, and Michael Gardiner was living just around the corner in Elizabeth Grove. Skinny, with orange hair, a feminine voice and a reputation for wearing dresses, he was an obvious target for homophobes.

Having eschewed his past relationship with Barry Lane, Wagner had by now become very vocal and macho about his newly found heterosexuality. He kept complaining to the

40

woman he was living with that he hated Gardiner because he was a 'fag who wore dresses'. He said that Bunting called him 'the biggest homo'.

Bunting had by this time left 203 Waterloo Corner Road and had moved to 3 Burdekin Avenue, Murray Bridge, a country town on the River Murray outside of Adelaide that had fallen on tough economic times and had plenty of cheap public housing for rent. He was still living with Elizabeth Harvey, mother of James Vlassakis, and her other sons by different men. Harvey was at that time very depressed and pumped full of medication. Bunting had used her to impersonate the voice of Suzanne Allen and also to make withdrawals from her Centrelink account.

Bunting and Wagner took Gardiner from his nearby home to Bunting's shed at the back of his house in Murray Bridge, where they strangled him, cut off his foot and stored him in a barrel in the shed. Again they followed the pattern of creating the impression he was still alive by telephone calls featuring a taped voice claiming to be Gardiner that said: 'Sorry about your stuff but I need the money. If you go to the cops, I'll go to the tax department.'

Michael Gardiner had been 'taken to the clinic'.

He had been 'made good'.

In the eyes of Bunting and Wagner, he was 'a dirty' who had been 'cured'.

But John Bunting was not happy. Barry Lane was talking too much. He had applied for emergency housing and was living in Adelaide in a suburb called Hectorville, with a mentally ill man called Thomas Trevilyan. Lane was running around telling everyone he knew that he was afraid of Bunting because he had helped him bury someone Bunting had murdered. He rang his sister and asked if he could live with her in Brisbane. He told his mother his life was in danger. His mother rang Wagner to see what it was all about.

Wagner drove to Murray Bridge to discuss it with Bunting. A month later, in October 1997, Lane disappeared.

~

Thomas Trevilyan answered the door at 34 Ross Road, Hectorville. Barry Lane had said he was too distraught to see anyone, and was lying on the couch when Bunting and Wagner walked into the room. His yellow-tinted glasses were wrenched from his head with the force of Wagner's grip.

'Hello, Barry,' said Bunting.

'Don't hurt me, don't hurt me,' screamed Barry.

'We're not going to hurt you any more than you hurt all those little boys. All those poor little boys you hung around schools and shopping centres and bogs waiting to trap.'

'You trapped me, didn't ya, Barry?' Wagner's hands were around Lane's throat.

'I loved you, Robert.'

'Yeah, sure, just like you loved all the others. You're a filthy, dirty paedophile, Barry. That's what you are.'

'I'm a transvestite. I'm Vanessa. You remember Vanessa. You know I tried to get a sex-change operation, Robert. You know that's the truth.'

'You're a dirty and a waste. And you're using up precious oxygen.'

Bunting moved to Wagner's side. Leaning over Barry, he growled, 'I told you not to talk, Barry. I told you to shut your mouth. But you couldn't.'

'I did, I did.'

'You told my wife about Happy Pants.'

'I didn't. Honestly, John, I didn't. Don't hurt me. Don't smash my face.'

'Worried about your face, are you, Barry? No need to worry about that, Barry. I've got other plans for you.' Bunting looked at

42

Wagner and nodded. Wagner produced a pair of pliers, which he used to squeeze Lane's toes.

Lane screamed and squirmed with pain. 'Don't hurt my face. Don't scar me.'

'Don't worry about your face, Barry. It's your toes we're interested in,' snarled Wagner. He was pumped up. Smug.

Every time Wagner used the pliers on Lane's toes and he screamed with pain, Wagner screamed louder, with laughter. 'Look,' he said to Bunting, 'he screams loudest when I squish his toenails, like this.'

Lane screamed and screamed, until he fainted from the pain. Wagner slapped his face. When he came around they made him ring his mother, abuse her and then tell her he was moving to Queensland.

At their invitation, Thomas Trevilyan joined in the final brutal punishment, and when Lane was finally dead, they rolled up his body in an old carpet lying on the lounge-room floor.

Barry Lane was on a disability support pension and therefore no paperwork was necessary for Centrelink to keep paying him the money.

After he disappeared, on two occasions, 20 January 1998 and 11 June 1998, a person giving the name of Lane gave Centrelink a change of address and collected the money.

Thomas Trevilyan had been diagnosed with paranoid schizophrenia and had already tried to kill himself twice. On 5 November 1997, two weeks after Lane's murder, he was found hanging from a tree down a steep embankment off the side of a road near Kersbrook, a country town close to Elizabeth.

The day before, 4 November – Melbourne Cup Day, to the rest of the nation – he was taken by Bunting and Wagner for a ride in their car.

After Barry Lane's murder, Trevilyan had been living with Wagner and his partner, and earlier that day he had been caught holding a knife and chasing the puppy belonging to Wagner's partner's daughter. When Wagner and Bunting returned home later that afternoon, Wagner's partner told Wagner that Trevilyan had to leave, that she wasn't going to put up with his crazy behaviour any more.

In the words of the prosecutor, 'He was clearly acting bizarrely and was too dangerous to be left to his own devices. He had also started to talk about how he had helped in Lane's murder. He posed a risk. Wagner tied him to the tree and Bunting kicked out the thing he was standing on.'

~

By the end of that afternoon, hearing it all for the second time, I felt as if I had been brainwashed. Or was experiencing a very serious case of déjà vu. Which, of course, I was. Wendy Abraham had done exactly as the judge had instructed and never varied from her original text.

Same words, same tone, same pauses. Almost automatic pilot.

No doubt a woman of great self-control, she resisted, if only to maintain her own interest, the urge to dramatise some of the more lurid passages the second time around. Her wig never moved a centimetre. Her hands never left the lectern, except to turn a page. How many hundreds – thousands, even – of hours must she have already expended preparing for this trial, piecing together every tiny detail?

Feeling the urgent need for a little distraction and refreshment, I stopped by the open stone courtyard in the middle of the Medina, where white umbrellas and a small fountain had created a taste of Rome in the middle of this antipodean city perched on the edge of a vast desert. A loud burst of male laughter focused my attention on one of the tables. This was clearly the place to be; it was full of young professionals showing off.

Sitting in the middle of the courtyard at the centre of a lively group was Christopher Pearson, holding court. By the look of his ruddy cheeks and the pitch of everyone's voices, they had clearly all been there since lunch and were planning to make an evening of it.

Christopher was in full flight – no doubt regaling his audience with some scandalous political story or anecdote from his eccentric life. He was one of the city's characters. He had gone from being a passionate Maoist to a card-carrying, neo-conservative, from a lapsed Anglican to a practising Roman Catholic, but he had always maintained his Evelyn Waugh sense of humour. And never denied his homosexuality. As he tells it in an essay in a book called *Double-Take*, in his first term of his first year at secondary school at Scotch College in Adelaide, a boy in his form asked him what he thought of girls' breasts. He'd replied that they were all right but boys' bottoms attracted him more. Evidently, apart from a boy named Ethel who later emerged as a transvestite and gangster's moll, Christopher was fixed in everyone's mind as the school's foremost poofter. In the early 1970s, before I met him, he became the lover of the State's leading lawmaker and classical poet, the Chief Justice, Dr John Bray. South Australia was the first state in Australia to abolish the law prohibiting homosexual behaviour between consenting adults in private.

When I saw the waiter deliver another two bottles of red wine to his table, I knew that this was not the proper time or place for our reunion. I slipped away to my room.

Thursday 17 October 2002

THE POLICE WERE STILL MYSTIFIED as to the identity of the murderer of the director of Mental Health Services and rumours in the media had reached fever pitch.

By lunchtime Wendy Abraham had reached that place in her opening address where she'd previously had to leave off, and we all resumed our frantic note-taking. I'll spare you the details of the next six murders. For now. If you've never been to a murder trial, then let me warn you about the boredom. Nothing to do with the content – it's the detail and the delivery. Forget anything you have seen on television. My favourites, *Law & Order*, *The Practice*, *LA Law*, even *Rumpole of the Bailey*, bear no relationship to anything I was witnessing here. The tedium lies in the language. You don't believe me? Then lean forward and listen. This is the Crown prosecutor speaking about the cover-up of the murder of the last victim, David Johnson, stepbrother to Vlassakis and the son of Marcus Johnson.

Ladies and gentlemen, on 19 May, 1999, Robert Wagner and James Vlassakis attended Marcus Johnson's flat and spoke to him. They told him that David Johnson was in a car accident, that he'd got a 13-year-old girl pregnant, that he, in effect, was in hiding and that they'd come to collect his clothes to take to him. Consequently Marcus Johnson allowed Wagner and Vlassakis to collect his clothes and they left the house with them in a basket. It is alleged that it was John Bunting who came up with that story. A version of this story was told to friends of David Johnson's. His voice had been recorded shortly before he was murdered. This recording was manipulated by using a Sound Forge program that Bunting had on his computer. On 11 May 1999 at 7.36 pm, Toni Freeman, a friend of David Johnson's, received a telephone call. This call was recorded. It's alleged that in this call the recording of David Johnson's voice was played to her. A very short call. This was followed by three other unsuccessful attempts by Bunting at 7.38 to call Toni Freeman's number. Even in the unsuccessful attempts, the attempts to play the voice are also recorded.

And then she detailed the transcripts of these recordings and the attempts by Bunting to contact Telstra to find out how you can telephone someone but prevent them from finding out your number. I know that the law depends on the nailing down of every fact and tiny piece of evidence in order to prove someone's guilt, but now I know why lawyers charge by the minute. It's boredom money. I was aching just from sitting still. Had enough? I certainly had. So, it seemed, had the judge. When the prosecutor paused for breath he jumped in and said: 'I think that's a good place to stop. We will resume at the same time tomorrow morning.'

These are the mundane but true facts of evil. These are the boring minutiae of lies and deception that the prosecution asserted Bunting plotted and executed in order to cover up not only twelve murders but his seizure of the victims' belongings and to ensure their continuing Centrelink payments. I was not a member of the jury and so I was free to make up my mind at any stage.

I knew they were both guilty.

I also knew that Salman Rushdie was wrong about Adelaide.

These events were not caused by things or people beyond our control. This was not the product of poltergeists or evil spirits, nor the exercise of power from beyond the grave.

These were the deeds of evil men, ordinary evil men, whether born evil or made evil, I didn't know, but I knew that they were mere flesh and blood, sitting here and now in this courtroom, less than a few metres away from me. If allowed, I could have touched them. They were men from a social underworld, an underclass, the extent of which I had never known existed, but they were not creatures from a supernatural world. That would be too easy. Nor were they instruments of the Devil. Demonisation would have been too glib an explanation.

I had gazed almost obsessively at the accused men while Wendy Abraham had calmly and dispassionately unfolded what was to be her case against them. She would prove, beyond reasonable doubt, that John Justin Bunting had murdered twelve people and in addition tortured, dismembered and, in some instances, skinned and defleshed them. Robert Joe Wagner, having already admitted to three of the murders, was charged with eight more. There was a third man to be tried, Mark Haydon, but that trial was to occur at a later date.

As the prosecutor had reeled off the list of the murdered victims, Wagner had looked around the room and Bunting had stared straight at the jurors. I had looked at the faces of Bunting and Wagner. The listing of the victims' names could, for them, have been the recitation of a shopping list. Their faces offered not a flicker of anything that could have been described as an emotion, let alone remorse.

~

Adelaide is an elegant city, resplendent with heritage buildings despite the ravages of the developers' bulldozers in the 1970s and 80s.

I had chosen to stay at what had once been the Treasury building, firstly because it was a short walk across Victoria Square from the Sir Samuel Way Law Courts, and secondly because I was curious to view its transformation from the original Adelaide Treasury to a serviced apartment hotel. According to its plaque, the original building had been constructed on the same site in 1839, only three years after settlement. It had been designed by George Strickland Kingston, who was the Deputy Surveyor-General. Every day on my way to the trial I passed his bronze statue on the corner of Victoria Square that faces Grote Street.

Safe inside the law courts' thick sandstone walls (the police still had no leads on Monday's shocking murder of Margaret Tobin, the director of Mental Health Services), I went through my notes and tried to get straight in my head what I knew from my research and had taken down from the Crown's opening address. The main problem for me in attempting to write my article was that the lives of the accused were so intertwined with those of the victims. Bunting was clearly the puppeteer, who found himself in the middle of a ghetto of damaged people whose lack of education or intelligence or stability made them easy for him to manipulate. And, in some cases, eliminate.

Friday 18 October 2002

STILL NO INFORMATION REGARDING Margaret Tobin's murderer but a formal statement from the premier, Mike Rann:

> Dr Margaret Tobin was internationally renowned for her commitment to the area of mental health and had occupied the position of Services Director for the past two years. She was instrumental in the reforming of South Australia's mental health system and championed the increased funding of accommodation and emergency help for the mentally ill, especially in the area of economic deprivation.

Someone who clearly had a mental health problem was hearing these words and congratulating themselves for getting away with murder. So far.

My last day of the trial. I must confess to being a little hungover. The week had taken its toll and I had gone, late the previous night, to a private dinner in a beautiful old bluestone villa deep in the heart of one of Adelaide's best suburbs, with some of my former colleagues from my lecturing days at the University of South Australia. My only stipulations were lots of red wine and no mention of bodies in barrels. They were more than happy to oblige. In fact, no-one really wanted to talk about it – which suited me, but I couldn't help thinking it was typical of Adelaide's endless capacity for denial. If this were a Shakespearean tragedy and Adelaide the lead character, denial would be her fatal flaw. Is it perhaps the fatal flaw of all Utopian idealists? Perfection is a hard taskmaster.

In 1994 when rumours that the government-guaranteed State Bank was billions of dollars in debt were confirmed, Adelaide's governing classes pretended not to know even though the dogs were barking it in the street. The good citizens of Adelaide wanted to believe the blue-eyed, blond-haired premier, who had gone to the best school, and who every day in his sober grey suit and black lace-up shoes stared into the faces of his critics and the television cameras and denied there was trouble in their little paradise.

The facts, when John Bannon – then both premier and treasurer – was finally forced to reveal them, showed a $3.6 billion debt. A million dollars a day lost for every year of his ten years in office. The press labelled him 'the million-dollar-a-day man.' The Royal Commissioner concluded that he had been 'dazzled' by the bank's former CEO, who had consistently told him there was no trouble in paradise, no trouble at all. As an 'old boy' of St Peter's College, Adelaide's most prestigious school, he has been declared a member of a protected species, even by his own critics. His supporters believe that, like King Lear, he is 'a man more sinned against than sinning'. His detractors just shake their heads and cross the street when they see him.

Not that anyone speaks about these things in public. Bad form, don't you know.

This morning it was the defence counsel, Mark Griffin's, turn to address the jury. Bunting never took his eyes off him, this slim figure in black, his wig perfectly placed, his tone matter-of-fact, professional, unemotional.

Mark Griffin was at pains to emphasise to the jury that the basic tenet of our legal system is a person's right to a fair trial. 'It is a phrase easily said but less easy to believe or apply,' he said. He went on to emphasise that the presumption of innocence is fundamental to the way our system operates and that they had to continue to remind themselves of that throughout the trial. The country had entrusted them with this responsibility.

> As a Jury of peers it is essential that you remain impartial. There is a tendency these days for people to immediately take sides on every issue. You must consider a verdict in relation to each count. The burden of proof is on the Prosecution. The defendant doesn't have to prove or disprove anything. There are no expectations on the defendant. Our primary job is to protect and defend a person's right to a fair trial as best we can. My primary job is to ensure that the Prosecution's case is challenged and tested. I will attempt to identify evidence and highlight the facts and address you on each count as to why we say that John Bunting is not guilty of each count.

Now it was the turn of Stephen Apps, representing Robert Wagner. He began, 'Members of the jury, Robert Wagner pleads not guilty to –'

Before he had even finished his first sentence a member of the press gallery who had stood up to leave suddenly fell down the steps, eventually scrambling to her feet in a daze of embarrassment. Everyone in the court stared at her, such is the relief of any distraction from the formalised rituals of justice. When she stood up, we all looked away, embarrassed at our own voyeurism.

If you believed in signs, it was an inauspicious start for Mr Apps and his client.

Apps continued: 'You may find that Mr Wagner is not guilty of murder but guilty as an accessory after the fact, assisting after the event.

'In terms of the allegations of torture, we don't expect you to view him with any sympathy at all. The issue is not a question of like or dislike. Your duty is to the State to try Mr Wagner fairly and I'm confident that you will do that regardless of your personal feelings for him.'

Justice Martin, resuming his pastoral tone of voice, turned to face the jury: 'Do let me know, if, as a group, you need a break. You may find all the hours of concentration make you very tired . . . [I'm exhausted already, I thought to myself. Thank God I never chose to study law] . . . Some days you may feel grumpy . . . [you can say that again, Your Honour. All hail to the judge. A learned judge. A wise judge.] . . . that's perfectly normal. Some days I will be grumpier than others, so too the counsel. Always remember they are like ducks on the pond. They may look very calm and unruffled on the surface of the pond but underneath that surface, they are all paddling like hell.'

A general titter arose from the courtroom, mostly from the barristers. The accused remained expressionless.

And then, the prologue being over, the play began.

The first witness was called.

'Call Brian John Kay . . . do you swear . . .'

While the former police officer from Forensic Services was giving his evidence and the defence counsel were cross-examining him to try to find some inconsistency, some hesitation, some chink in the armour of evidence, my attention was, as usual, on the accused. Their faces were turned towards the witness.

Two heads of close-cropped hair, two sets of spectacles, two birds on a wire.

At 12.45 pm the judge declared it was time to break for lunch. The trial would resume again at 9.45 on Monday morning.

'All stand.'

The judge left the courtroom first, followed by the prisoners and their armed guards. The first week of the trial of the nation's worst serial killers was over. The defence counsel and their assistants packed up their laptop computers and their bags of files, and the media lurched out of their benches. All of us desperate to escape.

~

The Sir Samuel Way Law Courts sit on the western side of Victoria Square, named, of course, after Queen Victoria, who had ruled over all the pink bits on the map. That included Australia. And still does. Queen Victoria's statue stands firmly centre stage in her square. She is solid and solemn in her lace cap and long skirt, and in her hands she holds the orb and sceptre, emblems of sovereignty. Whenever I look up at her imposing presence I feel I should be able to press a button and elicit a stirring rendition of 'Rule Britannia'. Adelaide's ruling classes would never approve of such a multimedia attachment to the statue, not because they don't keep up with such innovations but because they would consider it 'unseemly' and – well, 'common'. To be dubbed 'common' is one of the worst sins in Adelaide.

This city, capital of South Australia, was to be the jewel in the crown of what was planned as the perfect colony. When it was finally settled, its citizens never referred to themselves as a colony but rather as a province. From the very beginning it was important to them that, unlike all the other states, they had never allowed convicts among their number. They were descended from 'free' settlers, from the 'middling classes' lured by dreams of being part of the creation of a paradise, a perfect province, a radical Utopia.

Ironically, Edward Gibbon Wakefield, the man who planned the establishment of this perfect colony, did so while cooling his heels in Newgate Prison, having been incarcerated there for three years for abducting a schoolgirl heiress. It was his second venture in marital piracy. His biographer, the late South Australian writer Geoffrey Dutton, revealed that 'ten years earlier he had run off with a ward in Chancery, Eliza Prattle, who died in 1820 leaving him with a son and a daughter'. Coming from a background stock of Quakers and philanthropists (his cousin was Elizabeth Fry, the prison reformer), Wakefield used his time in prison to set about reading everything he could on colonisation, very much a hot topic in England at the time. So even from its very conception, this state was mired in contradiction and eccentricity.

When Wakefield was finally released from prison he gathered about him some wealthy and influential men, and in the leather chairs of their smoke-filled gentlemen's club, they created the blueprint for this state into which I was born and to which my forebears came, both sides of my family arriving within the early years of settlement.

Wakefield's plan was to invite only those people who could afford to buy land to settle there first and the labouring classes could follow when needed. So, in today's parlance, they bought 'off the plan'. In his book on the early history of South Australia, *Paradise of Dissent*, Dr Douglas Pike says, 'Wakefield was responsible for removing from immigration the stigma that had turned the middling classes against it. Where they had seen (and shunned) only a squalid traffic of convicts, paupers, fugitives and rum racketeers, he taught them to see instead solid opportunity and a civilising mission.'

From its earliest conception, South Australia – and its capital city of Adelaide – was based on the notion of perfection. As Pike says: 'like Plato, Wakefield had a vision of a perfect pattern of society laid up in the heavens. In a balanced community of enlightened citizens, with ever-increasing production, Wakefield promised no adoration of wealth, no oppression of the poor, no reason for political dissent'. In short, Pike notes, it would be 'the happiest state of society consistent with the institution of private property'.

And so, Adelaide, named after the wife of the reigning King, William II, was to be a properly planned town, which would gradually spread in a regulated pattern over the adjoining countryside. English society, arts and refinement could then be transmitted to its citizens in the shortest possible time. According to Pike, 'The new society would be a youthful projection of the old; familiar buildings, accents, decencies and institutions would remind the settler that although he had changed his address he was still among respectable people.'

And the society that developed was indeed a projection of the old. The Adelaide accent is noted for its long vowel sounds, for example, graaph, graant (for graph, grant), and the buildings are replicas of what was left behind in England. Perhaps the best example of its many contradictions is the fact that near or next to every church is a hotel, but even within the latter, adherence to certain 'decencies' is still a fixed part of the culture. Adelaide pubs were never the rough alehouses of the other capitals; in fact, the irony is that like the churches, many of the pubs – constructed of the attractive local bluestone – have now been converted to private housing or restaurants.

The word 'respectable' is a key word in understanding this city. Adelaide's sense of its own respectability goes to the heart of its contradictions, particularly in attempting to understand how such a civilised and cultured society came to produce a hidden underbelly of deprivation and depravity, ever-expanding ghettoes of deviance and dysfunction that had resulted in the enactment of the most horrific serial killings in the history of the entire nation.

The law courts are well positioned in the middle of the western side of Victoria Square between Grote Street, named after the radical philosopher and banker George Grote; and Gouger Street, named after Robert Gouger, the son of a Lincolnshire businessman. Gouger has been described as 'a civilised intellectual of great integrity, with some skill in music and an interest in natural history, ardently in favour of the civil and religious freedom which would exist in South Australia'. Grote is best known for proposing a secret ballot for voters, his plea being that the influence of wealth was no substitute for personal merit.

All the streets within the four square terraces (North, South, East and West) within which sit the four planned squares (Light, Hindmarsh, Hurtle and Whitmore) are named after some of the enlightened men who helped found the city.

The man who was entrusted with choosing the position and the laying out of the plan of the city was Colonel William Light. His statue now stands on Montefiore Hill overlooking the city square and the hills beyond, to which Light's bronze finger is still pointing. Below the statue is a plaque on which is inscribed words from his 'Brief Journal':

> The reasons that led me to fix Adelaide where it is I do not expect to be generally understood or calmly judged of at the present. My enemies, however, by disputing their validity in every particular, have done me the good service of fixing the whole of the responsibility upon me; I am perfectly willing to bear it; and I leave to posterity, and not to them, to decide whether I am entitled to praise or to blame.

A hard time poor Colonel Light had of it. He lived only two years after the colony was officially settled in 1836. Having planned what is generally regarded as the most gracious city in Australia, his last days here were fraught with tragedy. While

Light was waiting for his new house to be finished, the wood and reed surveyor's hut in which he had been living with his faithful companion, Maria, caught fire and burned to the ground. Destroyed with all his belongings were Light's portfolios of drawings executed during his residence in Egypt, the Iberian Peninsula and, of course, South Australia. Nothing was left of the private journals he had diligently kept for the previous thirty years. The loss of these precious journals and drawings broke his spirit, and when the governor held a special dinner in his honour, he was too ill to attend. He died with Maria by his side, shortly after moving into his new brick house in Thebarton.

Dutton records that in 1858:

> Light's old friend George Palmer [Palmer Place] sent a silver bowl to the Mayor and Corporation of Adelaide as a gift from himself, Jacob Montefiore [Montefiore Hill], Raikes Currie [Currie Street] and Alexander Elder [Elder Park and Elder Hall] with the following inscription:
> 'Presented to The Mayor and Corporation of Adelaide that they may thereout drink in Australian Wine to the memory of Lieut. Col. William Light, the first Surveyor General of South Australia, by some of the original founders of the Colony.'
> As a result, the Council authorised a sum not exceeding ten pounds to be expended in Colonial wine and biscuit in order that the citizens may drink to the memory of Colonel Light.

And once a year on his birthday this tradition is still carried out.

Fortunately for the councillors, the local wine is now among the best in the world.

Colonel Light was born the illegitimate son of Sir Francis Light. His mother, who was never married to his father, was variously rumoured to have been a Malay princess, a Portuguese half-caste or Eurasian, probably from Siam. If you look at the painting still hanging in the Adelaide Town Hall of William as a young soldier, you will see a man described by a friend as 'of medium height, sallow complexion, alert and handsome, a face cleanly shaven excepting closely cut side whiskers, black curly hair, brown eyes, straight nose, small mouth and shapely chin.'

In other words, he's sexy.

William's father had planned the city of Penang (the sister city of Adelaide), which had been established solely in the interests of empire and trade. William, though, had planned a perfect city to match Wakefield's high principles and social ideals.

For fifteen months prior to his decision to site the city of Adelaide where it now stands, Light had made maps and surveyed 150,000 acres with scarcely any skilled assistance, very little equipment and with constant interference from authorities and governors Hindmarsh and Gawler, who thought they knew better in such matters.

Dutton tells us that 'his sketch shows the town Adelaide in two rectangular blocks, the larger to the south and the smaller to the north of the river Torrens, the whole surrounded by a belt of parklands about a half a mile wide. In the heart of the open city, there was to be a large open space, Victoria Square.'

The theory most accepted is that his plan was based on that of an old Roman military camp. Savannah, in America's south, is a city whose plan is very similar to that of Adelaide. It, too, is based on the squares of a Roman military camp. It, too, has its secrets in the garden of good and evil.

Light laid out his city with a clear eye to its future. Wide streets, vast squares, all in an ordered rectangular pattern surrounded by the natural parklands with their galahs and magpies living happily among the gum trees and the pale summer grasses. The wide streets were to be balanced by noble and strategically placed architecture. The reason he wanted the streets to be so wide and straight was to prevent the dirt and crime and corruption that he had perceived to be flourishing in the dark back alleys of London's narrow, winding streets. Unfortunately, instead of putting up their premises along the wide streets provided, the local shopkeepers perversely crowded into narrow Rundle and Hindley streets – where they still are – because they wanted to be close to the river and the harbour road. Hindley Street to this day is painted with a somewhat seedy reputation due to its narrowness and number of night-clubs, massage parlours and strip joints.

Within only a year of South Australia's being proclaimed a colony under a large gum tree (still standing) at Holdfast Bay in Glenelg in 1836, Adelaide was a lively and well-established town. According to Dutton, Sir John Morphett (Morphett Sreet and Bridge) described the style of living as remarkably comfort-able. It is this word 'comfortable' that is still used most often by Adelaide residents. Morphett wrote that 'visitors from the sister settlements in Australia . . . are surprised at the style of our liv-ing and the tone of our society'.

Again, note the use of words like 'style' and 'tone', both given as important attributes of the city today. Margaret Whitlam, a former first lady to Prime Minister Gough Whitlam, when she visits, always describes Adelaide as very 'couth' – as opposed to 'uncouth.'

Morphett thought that, 'It would be no very difficult matter for a person to cheat himself into the belief, while visiting at the houses of some of our settlers, that he was only a few miles from London. The illusion would arise out of neatly, and in some cases, elegantly, spread dinner tables – well-cooked dishes – champagne, hock, claret and maraschino – the presence of some well-dressed and well-bred women – and the soothing strains of the piano.'

The tone for the life of the city, set from its very beginning, is still much in evidence. Adelaide is a city with a relaxed and elegant lifestyle, where the best food and wine are easily available and consumed on a daily basis, where intelligent conversation and radical ideas are valued, and whose Festival of Arts is considered the best in the country.

This is exactly the vision Light had firmly in mind when he first surveyed that hot, dusty plain and planned a city he hoped would produce the greatest good to the greatest number of its inhabitants.

In the 1970s another visionary, Don Dunstan, turned Adelaide into a powerhouse of political and social reforms that left the rest of the country gasping in its wake. Dunstan proved during his decade-long premiership that innovation could be popular and viable. His goal was to make South Australia the most sophisticated city-state in the southern hemisphere, with the highest quality of life.

He drafted and implemented the first consumer protection laws in Australia. 'Ordinary people have to be able to buy a house and a car and have protection if they are not treated fairly,' he said. Hot on the heels of this legislation was his abolition of all discriminatory laws regarding race, colour of skin or country of origin. South Australia was the first state to enable Indigenous Australians to live on their own lands and determine their own future with assistance from the state government. Dunstan's social democratic ideas were based on those of the British thinkers Harold Laski, Richard Tawney and William Morris.

It was Morris who influenced him to abolish the dress rules for Parliament. Dunstan had grown up in Fiji wearing shorts to work and was a firm believer that well-designed functional clothes suitable to the climate were an important part of 'the good life'.

However, when he wore pink shorts to a Cabinet meeting, the television cameras went feral. It was even reported in Zanzibar. His next attack was on areas in which the law was used to regulate behaviour where the 'crime' was victimless. He tackled and enacted homosexual law reform, sex discrimination legislation, censorship laws and what proved to be the most difficult and controversial of all, the Licensing Act, thus setting in place a tourism industry based on food and wine. The good life meant enhancing the intellectual life of its citizens, and Dunstan put a great deal of effort and funding into establishing permanent arts companies in theatre, opera and film. It was to Dunstan's Adelaide that I returned after several years working in London and he provided the model against which I judge all politicians. It was a privilege to know such a person and to witness what is possible if you have a clear vision of what you want to achieve.

~

At the end of the first week of the trial, having gathered more than enough material for my feature article, I returned to Brisbane, whose citizens I was talking to on a daily basis as the presenter of the morning program on ABC radio. Living in an apartment overlooking the Brisbane River in full view of the beautiful Storey Bridge, I thought about the fact that Brisbane had never been the radical Utopia of Light's Adelaide – far from it – but it had nevertheless eventually developed into a paradise of a different kind.

The long vowels of my Adelaide accent had taken a while for the Brisbane listeners to get used to as they were fiercely parochial, like all the inhabitants of the Australian capitals. I was called a Mexican (being from south of the border). Apart from the Indigenous inhabitants who had been in our country for over 30,000 years, we are an island continent populated by continuous waves of immigrants, most of us far away from our forebears' homes but nevertheless living a modern European lifestyle. Only just over 200 years old as a nation, we cling to whatever sense of belonging and roots we can find.

Brisbane had originally developed as an overflow from the convict settlement of Sydney, and its tropical climate in the north of this vast continent gives it a relaxed country-town feeling even while it spreads and surges ahead as a highly successful, sophisticated city.

I reminded myself that John Bunting had grown up here in one of its poorer suburbs. He had no doubt at some stage in his life spent time on the banks of this same river.

Sitting on my balcony in the warm dusk watching the little ferries go up and down the Brisbane River, I couldn't help thinking about another river called the Torrens. It wasn't much of a river – more of a creek, really – just like the one in Savannah that Johnny Mercer made famous in the song 'Moon River'.

I remembered, too, the English university lecturer, George Duncan, who in 1972 had wandered alone on its banks one night in search of company, only to be attacked by strangers, bashed and hurled into the river, where he drowned. He couldn't swim. The government held endless inquiries after his death and even flew in detectives from Scotland Yard to assist the local police, but they could never make the charges stick against the two vice squad detectives who were thought to be engaging in a bit of local 'poofter-bashing'.

If a city is planned to be perfect, if its citizens think of themselves as having the best possible life, if the expectations of a Utopia are ever-present, how, then, do they cope with its underbelly, with the serpents slithering about, unnoticed and disregarded on these hot, bright, plains of Paradise? How indeed.

II

UTOPIAS

June 2003

THE FEATURE ARTICLE HAD NOW grown into a book and although I had left Brisbane and was living back in Sydney, the trial of John Bunting and Robert Wagner continued in Adelaide. So, too, did the Adelaide Cabaret Festival, which was of far more interest to its citizens than a murder trial focused on what they considered to be what a bunch of low-life deviants had done to each other. It was, they said, all too gruesome for them to contemplate. Even if there hadn't been suppression orders, they wouldn't have wanted to know the details. At least, that's what they told me.

'Susan, why are you back home?'

'Well, I've decided to write a book about the Snowtown murders and . . .'

'Why on earth would you want to do that? How ghastly.'

'It's not just about the murders, it's about Adelaide and why they happened here and . . .'

'I hope you're not going to repeat all that nonsense about us being a murder capital; it's ridiculous. And wicked . . . And wrong.'

'Salman Rushdie did say that things go bump in the night here.'

'Nonsense. How long was he here? One week, for the Writers' Festival.'

'But Barbara Hanrahan always said there was something weird about this city.'

'Yes. Well. Barbara was always a little weird herself . . . talented . . . but, well, different . . . very different. Now, what are you going to see at the Cabaret Festival and when are you coming for dinner?'

I had many conversations along these lines. Comforting, really, to know that the worthy citizens of Adelaide had lost none of their certainties or their priorities. And none of their talent for denial.

In the Utopia of Adelaide, it seems, there is still no wish to recognise the basic fact that if there is good, there must be evil. Let alone talk about it. As my mother and aunts continuously reminded me in my childhood: 'Just because there are nasty things that happen, that is no reason to talk about them. Least said, soonest mended.'

I was looking after a friend's house in Dulwich, one of Adelaide's leafy, affluent suburbs that border the eastern parklands of the city. Although South Australian women were the first in Australia, and only the second in the world, to gain the vote, it was in the centenary year of 1936 that E.H. McEllister of Dulwich argued in a letter to the editor of the *Advertiser*: 'The sexes were ordained in such a way that the man is the breadwinner and the woman the builder of the home. Any frustration of this principle and we would merely become a race of neuters. In Spain today "equality" has reached such a state that women are fighting in the war alongside the men! What a disgrace to true womanhood and motherhood!'

In fact, it was here in Dulwich that Tony Blair, the Prime Minister of Britain, had attended primary school, when his father was a lecturer at the University of Adelaide. What does

Dulwich have to answer for? I wondered. As the twig is bent, so grows the man.

It was winter and the house was made of the traditional sandstone. I had forgotten how bitterly cold Adelaide's winter could be without the benefit of central heating. I immediately ordered a tonne of mallee roots and red river gum to feed the open fire in the living room.

Even though the sun shone nearly every day, the wind demanded an English overcoat. Every morning I ate my breakfast (scrambled eggs, bacon, grilled tomato, toast and coffee, all for $5.50 – you'd be lucky to get a cappuccino for that where I lived in Sydney) and read the city's only paper at the nearby coffee shop called Three Benches. In fact, its scrubbed wooden floors and tables reminded me very much of the schoolrooms of my childhood.

There were the usual singles and couples having breakfast on their way to work, but most astounding were the numbers of mothers with babies in prams, sipping their cappuccinos. The more I walked the streets of Dulwich, the more they seemed to appear from nowhere. Up and down the leafy streets, in sunshine and in shadow. Tribes of them. I felt as if I was in a movie set in the 1950s. Except the mothers were in smart tracksuits and runners, not skirts and cardigans. I did, however, suspect there was still the odd strand of respectable pearls hidden beneath the sweatshirts.

In the streets
The women come and go
Dreaming of cappuccino

The affluent twenty- and thirty-somethings had bought up the heritage houses and were renovating and restoring them as if their lives depended on it. Colonel Light would have been so pleased. It was for just these sorts of families that he had planned his city.

Meanwhile, in Victoria Square, the play continued, now inside the much-publicised, finally completed, specially equipped law court that had taken $3 million of taxpayers' money to revamp in order to cover the large number and range of evidence and exhibits. It was, after all, the largest serial-murder trial in the history of the nation.

Every day, new witnesses were called and more details of the murderers' secrets were revealed.

Every day the ritual followed its preordained pattern. 'Court stand.' In walked the judge. The court bowed. The judge sat. The court sat. The case resumed. Different witnesses. Same barristers.

The accused men were still sitting there, just as I remembered them, as cold and motionless as if they had been carved by Rodin.

Every day I sat there, listening and watching before delving down into the bowels of the building to the media room, where the transcripts of proceedings were kept. Every day I took copious notes, still trying to get my head around the endless details. The devil is in the detail.

In the meantime, the good citizens of Adelaide's leafy suburbs went about their usual business: birth and copulation and death, having dinner parties, being engaged in parish-pump squabbles and generally enjoying the pleasures and ease of passage that a city with only a million people provides.

But what about the citizens of the city of Playford? That city encompassed Elizabeth, the first of the planned satellite towns that were supposed to form the basis for a burgeoning industrial hub in the north, those towns where not only the victims but also the murderers had lived.

Like most of the people who had always lived in Adelaide's

inner suburbs, I never detoured off the Main North Road, which led ultimately to the lush vineyards of the Barossa Valley or the beautiful soft contours of the Clare Valley and endless opportunities to taste some of the best wines in the world. I had never known anyone who lived in Elizabeth and I still didn't. Elizabeth, to me, had always been a sad place. A city of shadows and lost dreams.

It did not begin this way. It began as a city of light and hope, a 1950s 'new town', a social experiment, another Utopia, intended to be a model community of working people who would migrate there to make a better life for themselves and their children. In the words of biographer Stewart Cockburn, 'Elizabeth was the most renowned achievement of the Housing Trust. It aimed at fulfilling the Trust's original charter adopted in the 1930s to provide housing for those on limited incomes and to use its programs to achieve social objectives on the one hand and assist the industrial growth of the State on the other.' It was the vision of South Australia's longest-serving premier, Sir Thomas Playford, my grandfather's political hero, who by facilitating the marriage of the State's Housing Trust to provide the housing and General Motors-Holden to provide the jobs, set out to create an industrial paradise for the working classes.

He named his 'city of tomorrow' Elizabeth, after the reigning Queen, not just because Adelaide had been named after her reigning Queen but because most of the migrants he hoped to attract to settle here would come from Britain. And they did. They flocked here. In his biography of Playford titled *Playford: Benevolent Despot*, Cockburn writes:

> Housing Trust recruiting officers who went into the industrial towns of Birmingham, Sheffield, Manchester, Leeds and Liverpool found that families contemplating migration were

strongly attracted by the sound of a new town named after the Queen of England in a country on the other side of the world. With guaranteed houses and guaranteed jobs, they signed up in their thousands. At one stage something like 80% of the entire population of Elizabeth was English-born. The Queen herself performed the official opening ceremony and did her best to pop in for a visit whenever she was on a Royal Tour.

~

On 16 November 1955 the Premier's Office issued the following statement: 'Not since Colonel Light, with foresight generations ahead of his time, made history with his plan of Adelaide, has a town in South Australia been designed on the scale of this New Town.'

I read this statement in a book I had purchased from the council offices in Elizabeth. I had finally dragged myself away from the warmth of the open fire in Dulwich and driven up the Main North Road; past all the new and used car yards, the Chicken Kings and the Pizza Huts and the McDonald's, past the long-defunct Gepps Cross abattoir where as children we used to hold our noses against the stench that seeped in even through closed car windows. Gepps Cross was the place where John Bunting, with no sense of smell, had slaughtered and carved up dead animals. Resisting the last-minute urge to continue on to wine tasting in the Barossa or Clare Valley, I turned left where a sign with a Tudor Rose had proclaimed the City of Elizabeth.

The book I had purchased contained oral histories from the Elizabeth community and was titled *Elizabeth: From Dusty Plains to Royal Names*. It detailed the lives of all the early migrants who had once worked so hard to make this place a paradise for their families.

I'd had a great deal of difficulty finding the building that housed the city's history unit, and had spent over an hour totally lost in the maze of streets, arcades and malls all named after the Queen's children, her relatives and her castles. I was trapped in a giant royal jigsaw puzzle. Fortunately, the girl who eventually, via mobile phone, guided me through the maze was a paragon of patience and politeness. Not like the tattooed, singleted, bearded driver who had tried to cut me off, and given me the finger. As his clapped-out Holden roared off, I saw that he had a special message taped on his rear window. It read 'Fuck the Queen, fuck God and fuck you if you're close enough to read this.'

Not exactly the kind of model citizen that Premier Playford had envisaged.

According to the oral histories, everything was developing pretty much to plan in Elizabeth during the 1950s. By 1960 it was the biggest town in the state outside Adelaide. The Housing Trust had built neat, tidy houses for the mostly British migrants, who rented them at a very reasonable rate. They were hardly suburban palaces but were far better than anything the mostly unskilled or semiskilled migrants could have expected in the industrial towns in Britain where they had been born. The new settlers mostly had jobs at the car manufacturing plants of GMH and related industries, their children were at good schools, the government had planted trees in all the streets and planned a city square based on British prototypes. They had even built English pubs and named them 'The Red Lion' and 'The Rose and Crown' to make people feel at home. It was a workingman's paradise. But as Playford's biographer, Cockburn, states:

> The promise and prosperity of the 1950's gave way to various
> economic problems in the 1960's. A lot of the newcomers
> inevitably found many things, especially the drab, flat
> landscape, before trees and gardens had matured, not to their
> taste. They complained loudly and earned the anti-British
> nickname of 'whingeing Poms.' The town which was to

have become the City of Tomorrow was increasingly seen as
a dumping ground for British migrants. The dream began
to turn sour.

Mark Peel wrote a book called *Good Times, Hard Times*, which
is an analysis of what happened to Elizabeth during the time he
grew up there. From the beginning Elizabeth was isolated and
physically separated from Adelaide. Peel says, 'Well into the
1970s the boundary between Elizabeth and "town" was marked
by empty paddocks, the Parafield airstrip and the persistent
stink around the Gepps Cross abattoirs.' He always knew that he
lived in a factory town, not a 'suburb' in the usual sense. The
majority of men and women who worked in factories did so
within a few miles of their home.

Elizabeth was always seen as an experiment, a place on the
margins of Adelaide.

Unfortunately, the increasing economic downturn and decline
in the mass car manufacturing industry in the 1970s created
widespread unemployment, and by the 1980s Elizabeth had
developed a reputation for being populated by a growing underclass of the unemployed and the unemployable. It became a city
made poor by economic forces outside of its control. Premier
Playford had purposely tried to attract unskilled and semiskilled
migrants from Britain, his motive being that they would all have
the same background and be content to work in the factories.
When the economic slump came and GMH sacked large numbers of workers, they found themselves unemployed, with
nowhere to go and no educational basis from which to retrain.
Their only solace was that everyone they knew was in the same
boat. They were all forced to rely on welfare payments and, as a
result, their government landlord, the Housing Trust, pressured
to maintain income, was forced to drop its rents rather than have
street after street of empty houses.

With the lowest rental rates in the state, Elizabeth quickly became a magnet for others who were unemployed or lived on single mother or disability pensions. In the shadows of those who still had employment, in streets where all the houses looked the same, spread the human debris, hidden in the ghettoes of the lost, the forgotten, the disturbed and the deviant. Peel says, 'By the 1980's Elizabeth was more of an embarrassment than a showpiece. The model community became a lesson about social breakdown.'

Playford would have wept for his lost Utopia.

~

It was into these ghettoes that John Bunting had slithered. In the village of rejects, it is easy to be king.

'Look for the Clock Tower,' the girl on the phone had said. 'You can't miss it.'

Feeling like Alice Through the Looking Glass, I wound my way through what seemed endless malls surrounded by green lawns and banks of red roses and suddenly, as if by magic, there it was, the Clock Tower, straight out of an English tourist guide. I looked up to check the time. The clock on the tower said twelve o'clock. Surely I hadn't taken that long. I really was Alice. The Mad Hatter would appear next. I checked my own watch, which said ten minutes past ten.

Clearly, in this city, according to the clock on the Clock Tower, it was always midday. High noon in the workingman's paradise. Bunting would have walked by this clock tower. Many times. So, too, Wagner. So, too, most of the victims. Everyone in this sorry, sordid tragedy would have walked past the Clock Tower, under which I was now standing. And it would have always have midday. Midday on the plains of Hell.

It had started to drizzle; a soft, damp rain.

Rain that nourished the native trees in all the front yards in all the little houses, trees that had grown crooked against the hot northerly winds in the blast furnace of midsummer.

Rain that clung to your clothes and your hair, enmeshing you in its dank web. Rain that reminded me of the clinging smell of rotting flesh.

Rain that muffled the anguished cries of those who had found themselves facing unimagined terror.

It wasn't just the sudden chill in the air, it was the hopelessness in the faces of the people slumped nearby on the wooden benches, it was the sadness in the eyes of the men in oversized grey tracksuits sitting, smoking, staring into the middle distance, that made me flee to the warmth of the car.

It was easy for me. I could drive out of here, leave it all behind, go back to affluent, respectable Dulwich, light a big roaring fire, open a bottle of red wine and get on the phone to tell my friends how ghastly and creepy it all was. But the people I saw in the malls, the people who had been enmeshed in Bunting's evil web, had nowhere else to go. They were trapped; like rats in a maze. They were constantly on the move, from house to house, from one dysfunctional relationship to another, the women trailing children from different fathers, the children easy prey for sexual abusers. This was where the cheapest housing was available, this was where all those people whose lives were as hopeless as theirs lived, this was the bottom rung on the social and economic ladder. The victims of Bunting and Wagner had reached the bottom of the barrel long before they were dumped there.

Inside the security of the car, I scanned the street directory and drove slowly along the streets in order not to become hopelessly lost. I wished the planners had followed Light's example and stuck to a rectangular pattern. I stared at the blank faces of the houses, at the driveways full of rusting cars, at the front lawns decorated with discarded shopping trolleys. There was not a single human being on the streets, even though the drizzle had ceased. Every house looked the same. Every house had the curtains drawn. Street after street of rented neglect and sameness. Statistics from the Australian Bureau of Statistics proved that it was among the most deprived parts of not just the state but the nation, second only to some remote Aboriginal communities. From the statistics I could find, the majority of the people were unemployed and on some form of welfare, it had the largest percentage of single mothers, the largest percentage of people on disability pensions. These statistics were a dark, unwanted, cancerous secret, except to those who lived there. Try as I might, no-one from any of the welfare agencies would talk to me about it.

How many times had I, too, driven past the sign that said 'City of Elizabeth', in total, wilful ignorance of what kind of lives human beings were actually living there?

Now that I knew what had gone on behind some of those closed blinds, I began to understand the sullen, blank stares of the people in the malls, of the people loitering outside Centrelink, of the teenage mothers dragging little children behind them.

There it was. A house that had once sheltered John Bunting. I stopped the car and peered through my side window. A small lawn. A tired garden. A closed garage door. A neat, small house. Nothing to distinguish it from all the others.

What did I expect?

A plaque? A burning cross? A tourist sign? The Salman Rushdie Award?

It just looked ordinary. As ordinary as the face of John Bunting.

I started the engine, turned on the wipers as the rain had begun to drum on the windscreen, and drove to the next suburb of Salisbury. Destination, 1 Bingham Road, where Robert Wagner and Barry Lane had lived a few doors away from John Bunting and his wife V.

The rain was pelting down on the windscreen by the time I arrived in Salisbury. It had preceded Elizabeth as a town and each had been determined to keep their separate identities. But it all looked the same to me. Same Housing Trust homes, same ragged front lawns. I parked right out front. Same blind windows. Same rusted car in the drive. I wondered who was renting the house now. The street was empty. More than empty, it was eerily bereft. This could have been acid rain streaming down my windscreen. This was *Brave New World* meets *Blade Runner*. I shivered, but not from the cold.

No point in trying to find 203 Waterloo Corner Road. The house had been demolished after all the bodies had been dug up from the backyard. The neighbours did not want to live with its legacy or its nosey parkers.

No point in hanging around at all, really, now that the rain with its steady downpour was clouding my view.

Not that there was anything new to see. I had already seen it all, street after dreary street, house after drab house. All the dreams of a working-class Utopia, swept into the gutters like the fallen leaves from the stunted trees that lined each side of the endless streets on the endless flat plains.

I felt sorry for the people who had worked so hard to make it the fulfilment of their dreams, the people who still lived and worked there, who sat on the community boards and committees, who had made a decent life, who still lived in hope. Others had made a hell in heaven's despair.

The streets of Hell have probably always been paved with good intentions.

~

The streets of Dulwich were glistening in the rain, the bitumen smelling like fresh tar. Four o'clock in the afternoon. Mothers with umbrellas held hands with small children in brightly coloured raincoats as they crossed the streets to the village shops. Wisps of smoke were already appearing out of the chimneys of large stone houses where fires had been lit early for children returning from school or retired couples settling down for afternoon tea before the five o'clock news on television.

I put paper and a match to the embers left from the morning, knowing how quickly the winter cold filled the corners of the large high-ceilinged rooms with their leadlight windows and plaster cornices.

An open fire, a deep couch and a glass of wine could, perhaps, take the chill out of my soul.

~

The next morning, sunshine streamed through the coloured leadlight of the bedroom window, making rainbows on the polished floorboards. It was a day for renewal, for reunion, for reconciliation.

'Dear boy.'

'Dear girl, is it you, and, if so, where are you?'

'I'm in Dulwich.'

'Dulwich! Good God. What on earth are you doing in Dulwich?'

'I'm writing a book about Adelaide and the Snowtown murders, and I'm looking after a friend's house while I do some research.'

'Good heavens. The things you get up to.'

The amused chuckle belonged to Christopher Pearson, friend for over twenty years, former *Adelaide Review* editor and now, like me, weekly columnist for the national newspaper the *Australian*.

'When are we having lunch? Today?' he asked.

'Why not? I need a good long Adelaide lunch after the things I've been working on.'

'Tell me everything over lunch at The Greek. It's in Halifax Street, just around the corner from my new abode.'

'That must save on taxis.'

Not only was Christopher notorious for catching a taxi across a room if he could, he often used them to travel to his weekend country house an hour and a half's drive south of Adelaide.

'It does indeed, dear girl. Must rush. Have to spruce myself up now you're in town.'

The Greek is an unpretentious café and restaurant with excellent food and even better wine at more than reasonable prices, none of which, knowing Christopher's legendary lunching habits, came as a surprise to me.

We started with an assortment of Greek dips and a bottle of Henschke's Mount Edelstone, one of the best and most prestigious reds from the Barossa region. The winery was started by Cyril Henschke, who was shot by his wife; she was never convicted, allegedly claiming she had mistaken him for the magpies. At least that's one of the stories Adelaide people tell visitors in hushed voices whenever they drink the wine, which deserves more than a moment's silence, just in appreciation.

'Is that story about Cyril Henschke true?'

Christopher is an encyclopaedia of knowledge, from the most trivial to the most arcane. An only child, he had been encouraged by his mother to accumulate information and knowledge with the same passion other parents expended on urging their children to excel in sport. Although stocky in build and with muscular legs from swimming in his youth, Christopher has always suffered from poor eyesight, which made hand–eye coordination difficult. Our individual backgrounds and upbringings are a study in contrasts. While he had been listening intently to Schubert sonatas, I had been perfecting my forehand in tennis. He listened to nothing but the ABC on the radio as a child; I never knew it existed. In my house there were only two radio stations: my mother's, which played popular music and daily serials like *When a Girl Marries* and *Portia Faces Life*, and my father's, which presented all sporting events, especially the horse races. If Christopher and I as children were characters in the novel *To Kill a Mockingbird*, set not in the South of Australia but the deep South of America, he would be Dill and I would be Scout. Typecast, I'm afraid, for life.

His body now a living testimony to his addiction to good food and wine, he has always been eager to urge others along the same hedonistic path. Not that I needed any encouragement to join him. I haven't picked up a tennis racket in years.

He had certainly spruced himself up for our hometown reunion. Clean white shirt, pressed trousers, navy reefer jacket and maroon woollen scarf. It was an English style suited to someone whose opinions and sensibilities were strictly those of Britain between the wars. And now I had even heard on the grapevine he had converted to Catholicism, like his hero Evelyn Waugh, attending Mass with devoted regularity. No doubt, like Waugh, he would have replied to anyone who queried his decision, 'Imagine, my dear, how much worse I would be without it.'

We had a lot of old conversational ground to cover and new turf to plough. The gossip, scandalous and definitely defamatory, was as delicious as the food. The lunch was long but did not extend into dinner like some we had shared. He insisted I come back to his house for a sherry by the fire. A sherry? Very proper.

He was living in a large two-storey traditional bluestone terrace overlooking one of the city's major squares. His former friend and lover, Chief Justice John Bray, thirty years his senior, had lived in a similar terrace until his death several years ago. In Bray's honour Christopher had organised a memorial fountain in the square opposite, together with a plaque inscribed with lines from Bray's most admired poem. It was fitting that

Christopher had decided to buy this particular terrace for himself and his mother. Writer Peter Goldsworthy, a close friend, lived nearby. He was also Christopher's doctor. Christopher likes to organise his life along the Adelaide grid of ease and convenience.

As with all his houses, he had filled this one with his eclectic and eccentric collection of antiques. The front room downstairs into which he ushered me had what looked like two huge totem poles standing like goalposts either end of the closed red velvet curtains.

'Good God, what are these?'

'Ah, my dear, they are a find, I can assure you. These teak pillars are from the head office of the Imperial Bank of India in New Delhi. They are Nandi bulls on the top of the carved capitals. In the corner there, in the white marble, is Vishnu, sharing the corona with Hanuman, the pig who saved the world. And there with his lyre is the statue of Orpheus, who, as you know, is the demigod of poetry.' Christopher always assumes that such knowledge is commonplace. Smiling at my blank expression, he said, 'Surely you remember these Regency farmhouse sofas?'

'The same ones I used to lie down on after a very long lunch?'

'The very ones. And the angels carved in 1770 for the Pondicherry Cathedral are upstairs. They have joined the long table from the First Fleet and the Tasmanian cedar bookcases.'

'I bet every available surface is covered in papers.'

'Yes, well, I do like to have things to hand.'

We sat either side of the fire in high-backed Georgian chairs while he poured two sherries into Spanish glasses he told me were made from Napoleonic crystal.

We steered clear of topics that we knew from many years of argument and discussion we would continue to disagree over; topics like feminism, the republic, religion and political ideology.

Is there anything left worth discussing? Well, yes. Adelaide, for the moment.

As a former, speech-writer (if only briefly) for the current prime minister, he was well connected in political circles and had been appointed by the current Federal Government to the Australia Council and the board of the Australian Museum. His mobile phone rang constantly with his many and varied connections around the country seeking or giving information. What we did share was a long history of loyalty to friendship, a special understanding of loneliness forged between 'only children' and an irreverent sense of humour. Besides, only the most closed minds prefer the company of those who always agree with them.

Even though he hadn't been born in Adelaide and had moved here with his parents when he was in primary school, he had chosen to live here, always.

I had never really asked him why until now. Probably it was because he seemed to fit the city. I settled back into my chair for a long dissertation from the sort of person who, when asked a question, attempts to answer in the form of an abbreviated doctoral thesis, in perfectly balanced sentences. When Christopher speaks, you can almost hear the commas dropping their weight like sinkers placed at the bottom of curtains to keep them perfectly straight. Half the time, in terms of my understanding, he might as well have been speaking in Latin. Sometimes, he was.

'I think that Adelaide – and this is not especially mean – gets a lot of its distinct character from its containment as a city-state, a village atmosphere, everyone knowing everyone. Everyone having the sense, like an extended family, of having to get on with everyone or else having to have public ructions that are public knowledge forever. In Barbara Hanrahan's article, "Weird Adelaide", there's a sense of people being on either the right or the wrong side of the tracks. But I read it differently. Having lived on both sides of the tracks in Adelaide, in working-class Bowden and at Mile End, not far from Rose Street where Hanrahan grew up, I think that, except in the very stodgiest of Adelaide dynasties and in the echelons of the super-rich who have been super-rich for four or five generations and continue to have servants, Adelaide was actually a surprisingly inclusive place. I think that the chips on a lot of young Greek men's shoulders about "skippys" and that Anglo-Saxon kind of thing, were relatively easily removed when they realised that they, too, could be members of parliament. They, too, could be self-made millionaires. That it was a permeable membrane and that, as a famous English historian said, the English class system, which is much more rigid and forbidding than ours, is as much a ladder as it is a scale. It's possible to climb it and it's possible to fall off it. If you work hard enough at your rehabilitation, you can become a Master at St Mark's College.'

We snorted in unison at this reference to former premier John Bannon. Christopher poured me another sherry and I settled back into the Georgian armchair . . .

'What I'm saying is because of the proximity that comes from having a main shopping precinct, one Festival Centre, one market and a number of restaurants where you're likely to bump into anyone and everyone you've ever known, or whoever wanted to know you or you wanted simply to avoid, there's a Noah's Ark quality to the place.'

My eyes fixed on a couple of beautiful champagne flutes on the marble mantelpiece.

'They're nineteenth-century copies of Georgian flutes.'

Nothing escapes his attention; least of all my lack of it. There was a limit to how long I could drink this sherry.

'Now, [pay attention, Susan, is really what he wanted to say] I think part of Barbara Hanrahan's sense of alienation from the other side of the tracks came because Barbara was a bit mad, or very eccentric. Fortunately, in this city we tend to reward such people.

'Culturally speaking, I suppose the most useful parallels are with those small German courts in the nineteenth century that were, in their way, quite small beer in terms of money, having been once rich and still able to attract Goethe, as we were able to attract J.M. Coetzee [the Nobel-prizewinning author] to live here. We're not in a position to abolish any taxes of any significance except on real estate, but something like that towards writers and artists would indeed be a gesture. But if you think Goethe and Weimar and attracting enough musicians of sufficient quality to Adelaide, you have the model.

'The reason why the State Bank disaster was such a significant fact in South Australia's cultural life was because it diminished the critical mass of middle-class professional people who made, sold or taught the arts, and could have done so anywhere in the world and chose to do it here because of the advantages of the climate and all the other advantages that the city has . . .

'So what the State Bank disaster did was to create a brain drain and a talent drain because we fell below that critical mass. But to young people to whom it had always been home and for people who liked it and were prepared to hang on, or people of independent means, and for people who were married and didn't work, not a lot has changed. There is a significant comfort zone. They say demographically that the rich are getting richer and everyone else is getting worse off. That's not true. What's happening is that the rich and the poor are both absolutely and relatively better off. It's the lower middle classes who are feeling the squeeze. It's the upper middle classes, I think, that have always been the most loyal consumers of the arts, patrons of the arts, followers of the arts, and their offspring. So it was the collapse of a particular echelon of people with a certain degree of education and cultural confidence.

'There's a sort of a measure that the Australia Council worked out about how people see themselves vis-à-vis the arts and how they see themselves as consumers of arts products and with what we're doing as arts activity. I think that Adelaideans probably, per capita, score higher, particularly on the passive consumption of the arts, than other people as a self-conscious, cheerfully-entered-into activity. And it's something that's part of a balanced diet. It's possible to be both an AFL maniac and an opera lover here and not be forced to internalise all those old divides between either one thing or the other.'

He paused to cough. Again. 'I'm sorry, but this cold I've been fighting seems to be getting the better of me.'

'You've been a good soldier to last this long.'

'I didn't want to let you down.'

'And you haven't. We've got plenty of other times to talk about this. I'll be back to follow the trial to its end.'

'I don't know how you can bear it, dear girl.'

One of the things I have learnt about relationships that have survived the test of time is that you don't have to say everything on a topic all at once. Besides, it was starting to get dark outside and I had promised myself my favourite South Australian whiting, cooked in a light batter, and some crisp homemade chips from what used to be my local Greek fish and chip shop on the Norwood Parade. They wrap it in white butcher's paper, which stops it from going soggy on the way home, especially if you tear a small hole in the top to sneak the odd chip. A glass of the Heggie's Clare Valley riesling that I knew was waiting in the fridge would be perfect in front of an open fire. Home comforts loom large in homecomings.

~

The next morning heavy rain was thrumming its favourite tune on the tin roof. Dragging myself out of the warm bed, I peered through the curtains to see the trees in the front garden making small waterfalls off their sodden branches. The rain hadn't stopped the parade of mothers. Under huge brightly coloured umbrellas they were still bouncing along the footpath with their prams, their runners squelching through the puddles, the little pink faces of babies barely visible beneath woollen hats.

In the streets
The mothers come and go
Dreaming of cappuccino

It was time for me to check up on what was happening in the court where I knew two men accused of horrendous crimes were sitting, side by side, in the dock.

I bowed to the judge and walked to the empty benches. No media contingent today. Not even a casual observer. This was the heavy slog of the law. Every point of evidence had to be covered accurately and in agonisingly slow detail in order not only to make the case for the prosecution airtight, but to ensure that after sentencing there were no grounds for an appeal. I listened for what seemed an eternity to a witness being questioned and cross-examined on material even I had heard several times before. The eyes of the jury were glazed, their bodies slumped into postures sculptured from long periods of sitting still. The accused, however, sat upright and alert, their eyes focused on the witness, concentrating on his every word. Wagner now had a notebook in which he was making the occasional jotting. He was illiterate when he had first been arrested but as one of the local journalists had told me, during the period he had been in prison he had gradually learnt to read and write.

As the trial ground on, I was reminded of the dictum that the journey of a thousand miles starts with a single step. And step by step, Wendy Abraham was making the case for the prosecution. Fortunately, I was not required to take every step of the journey, in person, with her.

While in the nearby coffee shop reading the *Advertiser*, I remembered a time when there was also an evening publication called the *News*. In fact, it was the very first paper that Rupert Murdoch owned. In 1952 he had inherited it from his father, Sir Keith Murdoch, and from there had built a global media empire with assets that today total US$42 billion. This global empire had begun in Adelaide; Murdoch had married his first wife here; had his first child here; and returned (until 2004) to its wide, handsome streets every year for his company's AGM, bringing with him members of his family and his top CEOs from around the world. In the beginning there was Adelaide, for the world's most powerful media magnate.

My eyes fell on the Cabaret Festival advertisement for Barry Humphries, who was doing a matinee performance that afternoon at Her Majesty's Theatre in Grote Street, only a stone's throw away from the café in which I sat.

Barry Humphries had made his career satirising everything that suburban Australia – including Adelaide – held dear. When I was seventeen I used to spend hours locked away in the bedroom of my boyfriend listening and screaming with laughter to Humphries' first LP record, *Wildlife in Suburbia*. We laughed until we ached and promised each other that we would each try very hard never to become a prisoner of the suburbs and never to miss one of Humphries' performances. Ah, the idealism of youth.

Gripping my umbrella firmly in my hand against the wind and driving rain, I staggered around the corner to the theatre, mindful of the advantage of a small city where everything you need is only walking distance away. As I stood in the queue for the box office, an Adelaide matron of indeterminate age – well-dressed, sensible shoes, recently coiffed grey hair – called out to me.

'Hello, Susan, are you back home to live or for a visit?'

I stared hard at her but couldn't recognise her face. 'Oh, you don't know me, dear. I used to see you on television.'

I smiled and said, 'Just home for a visit.' She nodded and gave a friendly wave. Several other women of her age smiled at me when I was finding my way to my seat. Another advantage of having grown up in a small city where people have seen or heard you in the media is that they always feel they know you. Familiarity gives you a sense of belonging, of having roots in the local soil. It may be sentimental or even illusory but it is agreeable and comforting. Like Vegemite on toast.

Barry Humphries, although an expatriate, comes home to Australia regularly enough never to lose touch with the material that fills his shows. My program featured a photo of his creation Dame Edna Everage resplendent in a purple Thai silk gown with matching winged glasses, wearing one of her most wicked and lascivious grins. The title of this show was *Back to My Roots*. You and me both, Dame Edna.

While I was familiar with a lot of the characters and the material, Humphries' sparkle and sheer energy never ceased to amaze me. The final sequence of the show starred Dame Edna and various people plucked mercilessly from the audience. This was always the most successful part of the show because the audience squealed with delight at the ways in which Humphries embarrassed and satirised the audience members on stage with him. This afternoon the entertainment involved Dame Edna squeezing out some personal family information and then proceeding to ring, from the stage in front of a live audience, a relative of one of her selected victims. During one of these hilarious phone calls, Dame Edna said on the phone to the mother of one of the women on stage, 'I love Adelaide, it's such a wonderful city,' and the woman on the other end replied, 'But don't tell anyone, will you, it's our best-kept secret. And we like it just the way it is.'

And I thought, I've been hearing that since I was a child.

On the one hand, the good citizens of Adelaide want it to be prosperous and successful as a modern twenty-first century city; on the other, they don't want anything to change, and they certainly don't want large influxes of outsiders discovering how wonderful the lifestyle is and coming to live here.

Adelaide is a secret paradise but, more importantly, *their* secret paradise. To keep this precious secret was almost a sacred bond between its citizens.

From its very beginnings, this city had seen itself as a family and believed that a close family never told its secrets to outsiders. That was what made, and more importantly kept them, a family. To spill the family secrets was tantamount to treason, especially in a city-state that considered itself a Utopia. If, as the psychiatrists tell us, you are only as sick as your secrets, then at times Adelaide has been very sick. Secrets, no matter how tightly held, have a way of bursting out of their dark hiding places and exposing themselves for all the world to see.

~

It was time to visit Snowtown. And its bank. But first I needed to spend a few hours with one of the sons of the original OAF (Old Adelaide Families), a man who, as a genuine descendant and member of this city's traditional ruling class, is warm and open, has absolutely no taint of snobbery or pretension, does not harbour secrets, has never belonged to the elite membership of the Adelaide Club and is, in my view, a worthy heir of the people who had first settled this city and set its values and standards. Now that the anthropologist in me was controlling the hometown girl, I wanted to explore a life lived on the right (as opposed to the wrong) side of the tracks. You would recognise Kym Bonython's style even if you had never met him. He's still good-looking in his eighties, his clothes are English county – comfortable, understated but of the finest cloth – his smile is open and engaging and you know from the moment you look into his eyes that there is no hidden agenda, no angst, no neurosis, no need to prove anything to the world. He is a man totally at ease with himself in any company. A totally Adelaide man.

I knew that Kym Bonython has three major lifelong passions, which he continues to pursue: art, jazz and riding his motorbike. Like Colonel Light, he lost all of his valued possessions when a bushfire destroyed his family home. Even though he rebuilt the house and continued to live in the Adelaide Hills, he eventually moved to an elegant but much smaller home in North Adelaide. From the outside the house appears to be just another well-kept bluestone villa but once you are inside, the paintings on every available wall space, the sheer comfort and quality of the furniture, signals a natural style that surpasses interior design or *Architectural Digest*.

We sat in his book-lined study, side by side on a deep, comfortable couch and as he began to talk about his life I realised that even though I had known him reasonably well when I lived in Adelaide, we had never discussed his life's history. He was so friendly and unassuming, it would never have occurred to him to tell me about it.

We started with his first name.

'My family are originally of Cornish descent and I was named after Reskymer Bonython, who was Sheriff of Cornwall in 1620.

'The original family fell on hard times and one of the family, a lawyer, tied a sheet around his neck and hanged himself on the veranda at Gray's Inn in London. Other members of the family went to live on one of the islands off the coast of Canada. That proved to be, for some reason or other, not satisfactory and they came back to England, by which time an Alfred Bonython had come to Adelaide and lived on the side of Mount Barker in the Adelaide Hills. No doubt he recommended to his brother that they should come here also. So his brother, George Bonython, who was a master builder, came out to Australia in 1854 bringing with him five-year-old Langdon Bonython, my grandfather, who started off at sixteen as a copy boy at the *Advertiser* and, by the time he was thirty-seven, owned it. Mainly because, I understand, he'd done some pretty prudent investment and mining in South Australia. He sold it, in about 1930, to the Murdochs. Grandfather always used to boast that nothing appeared in the *Advertiser* unless it passed his personal scrutiny, but I do remember from my youth one thing that escaped him. There was an advertisement in the real estate columns for a house for sale and in the blurb it said, "This house is ideally situated at the end of a long avenue of red bums." He missed that one.'

When Kym laughs, his shoulders shake. It's important to him that he entertains whoever he is talking to; for him conversation is an art, not an information exchange.

'My grandfather was a very God-fearing, kindly man. We were Methodists and we used to go to church regularly every Sunday. I never heard my father swear or tell a dirty story. I do remember that during the Depression, Grandfather used to have queues of unfortunates lining up outside his office in the *Advertiser* and he'd give them food vouchers. I never did get the definitive answer to whether he provided the money to build Bonython Hall because they wanted to stop Pulteney Street from going through the middle of the university. But I do know that one of the little quirks of Bonython Hall is that the floor has got a slight slope on it because it's supposed to stop people from dancing there.'

I suddenly remembered that old joke that goes . . . why don't Methodists ever have sex standing up?

Answer . . . Because it could lead to dancing.

Kym was enjoying his reminiscences, and had moved on to his passion for racing motorbikes.

'Speedway racing actually started in Australia in the 1920s and it ultimately spread around the world. Mother took me once to the speedway but it wasn't her scene, so thereafter I used to go every Saturday night with the family of my father's secretary. I was an avid speedway follower until the war, and then after the war ended, I went on to the land at Mount Pleasant, in the Adelaide Hills. While I was there the opportunity came to bid for the lease on the existing speedway, a place called Rowley Park. It was an old disused brick kiln, a hole in the ground in the industrial suburb of Bowden. I bid for it and got the lease and started competing as a driver in what we called speed cars, they called them midget cars in America. In its day, Rowley Park was internationally known in speedway circles because every year I used to go overseas and select competitors and cars and motor-bikes to come to Australia in their winter months to race here. I always used to say that when I die I want my ashes scattered over Rowley Park so that the public who used to boo me – good-naturedly, I think – would have to pick me out of their teeth. But they've spoiled all that by building a housing estate over it.

'Rowley Park was great. I used to sell meat pies, cakes and programs as well as compete. Sid Nolan [Sir Sidney Nolan, the artist] came one night and we were going the next day to Alice Springs while he looked around with a view to painting new pictures. But I had an accident and went to hospital instead.

'As for my passion for art, I was lucky inasmuch as my mother always had tastes ahead of her contemporaries. I must have inherited my tastes from her. I opened my own gallery in 1961. My wife Julie's family came from a property beyond Broken Hill and in the early 1960s I was asked by the Shell Motor Company to mount an art display in their new lubritorium. Wherever I went I saw pictures by somebody called Pro Hart and I said, "Who's this Pro Hart?" I was introduced to Pro and when I gave him his first exhibition, Barry Humphries opened it.

'Even when I moved to Sydney and had a gallery there, I pined for Adelaide. I missed the ease of getting about. You can be in the centre of Adelaide and then be at Mount Lofty in the Hills or on the beach at Glenelg in twenty minutes, which would be unthinkable in Sydney.

'When I was starting my collection I'd go to artists' studios, and so many of them said to me, "Why don't you open a gallery in Adelaide?" So I opened my gallery in Jerningham Street not far from here. I made a practice of never buying the eyes out of an exhibition before the clients had a chance to buy. My collection was largely made up either of paintings that people hadn't wanted to buy or, in some cases, when I heard of a promising artist and I'd go out to look at their work, I'd buy something from their studio and then arrange an exhibition the next year.

'I'm going to a grandson's engagement party in a couple of weeks in Melbourne and I'm looking forward to going to an exhibition there because one of its main exhibits is a Sid Nolan aerial view of central Australia I first bought from Peter Jones Gallery in Sydney in 1950. When Nolan was having his first exhibition in London he borrowed that picture to show there and it was the only one that the Tate Gallery wanted to buy and he begged me to let it go, which I did.

'Soon after, Nolan wanted to buy a Kombi van to travel around Greece and Italy, to go painting. I gave him five hundred pounds to buy the van and I could take paintings at a nominal hundred pounds each. Two of those pictures have already made over a million dollars each and I probably sold them for ten thousand dollars.

'I'm not as wealthy as some people make out. To do what I've done over the years, like building the gallery in Sydney, I've had to sell off some of my things. If I hadn't sold them and just kept them on my walls at Mount Lofty, they would have been destroyed in the fire. The year after the bushfire, during an Adelaide Festival, Barry Humphries had an exhibition in

Adelaide and one of the exhibits was an empty bottle with about an inch of ash in the bottom. He called that "Kym Bonython's art collection".'

He laughs heartily when he tells me this, illustrating not only Humphries' black sense of humour but the fact that Kym's is still in fine form.

He took me into the dining room, which was wall to wall with paintings, and showed me an architect's drawing of what the original house had looked like. His father had bought it in 1917, three years before Kym was born, and when his mother died Kym bought it. I also saw the picture of his namesake, Reskymer, the Cornish gent.

Just before I had knocked on the front door, I told him, I had heard jazz bursting through the front window. He said that's why he likes living in a house rather than an apartment. He still likes to play his music loudly.

'When I was a pilot in the war I used to carry my gramophone and records with me. I was more likely to die either racing to meet the latest girlfriend or else carrying my records and putting them into the trench before I got in. I have crashed four aeroplanes, been gored in both legs by a bull, spent over a year on crutches when my hydroplane blew up and been injured in countless speedway accidents. I said, "The good Lord is obviously saving up something particularly horrendous for me." I used to say this, until some woman said, "What, you mean like old age?" I said, "Yeah, that's right." The most horrendous thing of all. I did feel I'd led a charmed life.

'I was never a part of the so-called Adelaide Establishment. I inherited some of the advantages of being a member of the Bonythons but I like to think that my family, in the main, have done things well. And that we haven't been too avaricious. My grandfather was noted as a philanthropist, and helped university and education in addition to contributing to things like building a section of Parliament House. I like to think we haven't hurt people on the way. Admittedly, my grandfather was a wealthy man but he didn't keep it all to himself. He spread it around in things that he believed were worthwhile and people are still enjoying the benefits of that generosity.'

Kym said this with great seriousness, as if such sentiments were not readily understood by members of a younger generation schooled in the 'greed is good' philosophy.

I remembered my grandfather telling me that during the Depression in the 1930s, which hit a small city like Adelaide particularly hard, the government was finding it hard to pay the teachers' salaries. The Bonython family quietly used their own money to help pay the teachers. This was not just 'noblesse oblige' – this was a deeply felt responsibility towards those in the community who, through no fault of their own, were not as fortunate as the Bonythons. It went to the heart of the ideals that had formed the ethos of this city from its earliest beginnings. 'The greatest good for the greatest number' was never just empty sentiment. This Utopia had to exist for everyone who lived in it, regardless of wealth or status.

Kym had used his privilege and wealth to explore his passions and in so doing had expanded the pleasures and tastes of people less privileged. Whether it was racing motorbikes, or selling pies and tickets at his speedway, or exhibiting the latest Australian art in his gallery, or using his prize money to finance a tour by Dave Brubeck, it was all the same to him. There was never any notion of elitism or snobbery, only shared pleasures.

Adelaide has never lauded individual wealth for its own sake. The kind of conspicuous consumerism, the flaunting of huge houses and big cars which has characterised the larger capitals like Sydney would still be thought vulgar in Adelaide.

As I was waving goodbye and driving away, I thought how strongly that early character of his ancestors and all they had wished for their city of Adelaide was still present in Kym, almost like a genetic stamp. The eccentric sense of the individual's right to express himself balanced by the responsibility to give something back to the community, the lack of all ostentation, the love of both sport and the arts, the importance of being amusing and charming when in the company of others, the stoicism when disasters like bushfires strike . . . and then my mobile rang. It was Kym. He was apologising for not offering me a cup of coffee.

'Julie's away and I had the housekeeper set it all up and then got so carried away with talking that I totally forgot. I am so sorry for being so rude. Please forgive me.'

Add Adelaide manners to that list. Don't mock. Genuine manners are rare these days.

~

Snowtown is 180 kilometres north of Adelaide but unless you were going there to stare at a disused bank whose vault had once stored barrels of decomposing bodies, you would never bother. Once a thriving wheat-belt town, its grain silos stand empty by the railway station, rusting reminders of inexorable economic change. Underneath the sign that says 'Snowtown' is an advertisement listing the town's available services. 'Butcher' is the first on the list.

The sun was shining as I drove up the main street but the town seemed deserted. There were not even any cars parked outside the only pub. All I needed was an old ball of tumbleweed to come blowing past to convince me it was an empty MGM movie set. I was tempted to look behind the facade to see if there was anything there. I stopped immediately in front of the now-infamous bank which, unless you knew its gruesome history, looked just like every other small branch of the State Bank, closed due to 'market forces'. Its innocuous exterior with its green shopfront tiles and boarded-up windows gave no clue that its interior once housed the remains of the worst serial killings in the nation's history. I walked down the red-brick side of the building to the back gate, which was propped open with a handmade sign that read, 'Sheryl's Bric-a-Brac. Antiques, gifts.'

I called out a hello and an elderly woman appeared.

'Are you selling antiques here?' I asked.

'Well, not here exactly but round the corner and further down the street a bit. I'm going there now if you want to follow me.'

'Thanks, but I've got to get back to Adelaide. This is the bank where the murders happened, isn't it?' I thought I'd better check, now that I actually had a member of this poor, blighted community standing before me.

'Yes,' she said, looking somewhat embarrassed.

'I'm sorry . . . I'm a writer,' I said, in a pathetic attempt to convince her and myself that I was not just another ghoul come to poke my nose in.

Perhaps I should follow her and buy some useless piece of bric-a-brac just to give her some income, I thought. It was a damning legacy for this small town, forever branded through no fault of its own as a place of torture and murder. Perhaps they should make themselves a tourist destination and run organised tours of the bank's vault complete with 'I survived Snowtown' T-shirts and gift mugs. But that is not the South Australian way.

Of course, as soon as I shut myself in the car the thought of what had happened in that bank was so chilling and repulsive that I put my foot on the accelerator and left Snowtown behind, a diminishing reflection in my rear-vision mirror.

As I reached the outskirts of the city, a billboard reminded me Adelaide was in the middle of its Cabaret Festival.

Steve Ross, the international singer famous for his Cole Porter renditions, was performing them tonight in my old home town. The last time I saw him was in the celebrated Oak Room in the Algonquin Hotel made famous by Dorothy Parker and the other wits at the Round Table lunches. It was a far cry from Snowtown. Although both Cole Porter and Steve Ross had grown up in small country towns far removed from the glamour of Broadway. Steve Ross was in fine form and as I listened and laughed along with the Adelaide crowd, I was reminded of the power of music to help human beings transcend their fears, their hurt, their anger. I thought how fortunate I was to be able to wrap the magic of music and the wit of clever lyrics around my shoulders like a protective cloak.

None of the murder victims had ever experienced that joy or that privilege, such was the impoverishment of their lives. Nor, I'm sure, had the murderers.

~

At the beginning of the cleavage of those soft bosoms called the Adelaide Hills there is a peak called Mount Lofty, but mostly they are soft and undulating. At the bottom of these hills, amid a landscape of gullies and a waterfall where the ferns are thick and the foliage lush, is the home of Pam Cleland, Adelaide's most outrageous lawyer. Retired now but holding a different kind of court every night to the, mostly young, lawyers who call by for a drink and a conversation on their way home from work, Pam is legendary for the wild and exotic parties she used to throw for visiting artists, dignitaries and Adelaide's chattering classes. Premiers, international ballet dancers and chief justices were among the many guests often to be found naked in her spa or romping among the ferns. Pam always preferred not to wear clothes except when in court, although legend has it that she once appeared in court in nothing but a fur coat in the middle of summer.

When she opens the door I note that she has retained her petite figure. She is not naked or wearing a fur coat. She is dressed in a sweater, black leotards and high-heeled black shoes.

It is a Dorothy Parker face. Pert and amused. In her hand is a glass of champagne. She says that when you get older and your metabolism slows down, you can choose to eat or drink but you can no longer do both if you want to stay slim. For her, there was no choice. Red wine and champagne were always going to be the winners in that contest. So, what had she eaten for lunch? (I want to know just how much you have to deny yourself.)

'Today I had a small can of salmon, a small tomato and a few tinned peas.'

'That's it?'

'That's it for the day.'

'Surely that can't be healthy?'

'Well, I'm the one burying my friends, unfortunately. Anyhow, I know when I'm going to die. I've only got eight years left to live. My mother died at eighty-four and I think that will about do for me. I'm nearly seventy-six. Pretty old. It'll do. I've had a lovely time. A gorgeous time.'

I'd grown up hearing about Pam's notoriously scandalous parties and always regretted that I was not of her era. I wondered aloud why there were so many eccentrics in Adelaide in her day.

'I don't know. So many people were personalities in their own right and I don't find that as much now. I went to the University of Adelaide when I had just turned sixteen and it was full of marvellous people who knew nearly everyone in every profession. Now you're lucky if you know the people in your own year. It was the size of an English village, so eccentrics were protected.

'The reason I went to university was because I was sexually assaulted by my Uncle Ross when I was eight. It put me off the whole male sex until I was twenty, so I wasn't interested in men, or making a so-called good marriage, as a result of which I stayed at the university for umpteen years. Did an Arts degree and a Social Science diploma and then went over to Sydney to do an almoners' course until Dad got sick and I came back. I wanted to do higher maths but I thought that was a bit beyond me. And then I did law. I never intended to practise it. But it was very fortunate because Roma Mitchell [the first woman to be appointed to the Supreme Court in Australia and the former governor of South Australia] was around in those days and she encouraged everyone.

'Eventually I got a job with the ABC as a typist. They didn't ask me if I could type and I thought I'd be in a room of my own and if I typed with one finger no-one would notice. Anyway, when they saw I couldn't type they took pity on me and gave me a job in the records library. Then I went teaching at Wilderness [a private girls' college] and I had to teach anything they didn't have a teacher for, like chemistry, which I'd never done, and needle-work, which I was excruciatingly bad at. Eventually the need for money made me practise law and I did it for thirty-five years.

'I've always been a great reader. When I went to the university at sixteen I was mad on the pursuit of knowledge, just for its own sake. I wanted to read and study anything I possibly could and then eventually, after I decided I had to practise law, the only thing I ever read was law books and astrology magazines.

'When I was a child we lived behind the Mitcham Council Chambers and I've always been scared of the dark because I lived in the sleep-out. It was the Depression and there were always hobos looking in the window, terrifying the wits out of you. And also there were wavy trees and a lot of birds in them going "mopoke, mopoke". Still am scared of the dark. I don't like going out at night.'

We were sitting either side of a small desk, sipping cham-pagne, looking out of a huge window overlooking a tropical paradise.

'I planted most of these plants forty years ago. My neighbour is camp and he's got a thousand transvestites living with him. It's been delicious fun having them there. He's painted the front door and all the walkway pink, it's totally demented.'

I asked her why she was so keen on walking around naked.

'I was brought up a very strict Methodist and when I got undressed at night my mother made me pull my pyjamas up under my clothes. When I got away from Mother I didn't want to wear any clothes ever again. So we tended never to have anything much on. Once when we were all roaming around and dancing without our gear on the police came because our music was too loud. I put an academic gown on to see the police. It wasn't a great sexual orgy scene by any means, although I can remember having about nine people in our bed and no-one wanted me so I fell off the end. But it wasn't primarily a sexual scene, it was just enormously relaxing, with a lot of music and fun.'

As she continued to top up my glass I asked her why she loved Adelaide so much.

'It's the marvellous light. Light is very important, you know, think of the Beatles' "Here Comes the Sun" and the metaphysical poets, "I saw eternity the other night, like a great ring of pure and endless light." It's all to do with light, we're dependent on plants for our life and they're dependent on light for photosynthesis. I love light. I've just come back from Kangaroo Island and it's so beautiful there watching the sun come up over the horizon.'

And apart from drinking champagne, what did she do all day?

'I'm totally indolent. I read. I'm right back to where I was at sixteen. I just like reading anything I can lay my hands on to find out what people are thinking. I only read things that were written after 2000. I don't want to read old classics, I want to find out what people are thinking right now about everything.'

Of course, given the sexual abuse claimed to have been

suffered by the murderers and many of their victims, I couldn't help thinking about her uncle's sexual abuse and about how prevalent she thought abuse had been at that time.

'I would think one female in every three was sexually abused by about the time she was ten. I didn't mind terribly much as long as he brought me a box of chocolates. But if he came without his chocolates it was a lousy time. My mother used to say, "Father and I are going out and Uncle Ross will look after you." I thought it was all too boring. Once I was appearing for someone in the district court who'd sexually abused someone and I said to the judge, "Look, I was sexually abused when I was eight and I didn't turn out strange." He looked over his glasses and said, "I don't know about that, Miss Cleland." '

She laughed even louder than I did. A marvellous quality, the ability to laugh at yourself – but what was the most important human quality? She didn't pause for breath. Or even a drink.

'Enthusiasm. When I learnt watercolour painting from Gwen Barringer, she said, "You've got the most important thing of all, you have the kind of enthusiasm that comes from never knowing what's going to happen next." Even now in my geriatric dotage I always think something new will happen. You never know what new person is going to come over the horizon. Or what new feelings you're going to have. Or even what new thoughts. You think you've thought everything out but you can totally change your mind overnight.'

She stared at me with the kind of intensity only felt by people for whom life had always seemed rich with possibilities, with adventures. The opposite of those kinds of riches was the impoverishment of the lives lived by the murder victims. It wasn't just about money, it was about a wealth of spirit. Whatever her Uncle Ross had done to her, she had found the resources to cope with it. Was this a class thing or just her individual way of dealing with the world?

She said the abuse had put her off men but, despite affairs with women, she had eventually married. 'Fred was an enormously interesting man. He was a very good scientist and he was very highly read. His father said he was the greatest dilettante that had ever lived. The male side of his family came from Austria and his mother's side from Scotland, and they were very interesting people. I met him at a party, it was just one of those things.'

An affair was one thing, but why bother to marry?

'Mainly because of Mother's poker friends. They said to me, "You're living too near to that man and it's not right." In those days you didn't do that. I married him in 1960. Divorced him in 1970. Lived de facto with him until 1986, then one Sunday morning he said, "By the way, I'm leaving you. I'm going to live in Sydney." He went away for two months and then rang and said, "By the way, I'm coming back again." It's terribly complex. I liked him and I married him again in 1990, thirty years after the first marriage. There was never a dull minute with him. I don't think I've ever been bored in my life, ever.'

Another bottle of champagne launched a discussion about her parents. 'My mother was a bit difficult with her Methodist ways. I went off to America, and Mother being a strict Methodist, I didn't tell her the truth, but I went off with a Catholic nun, who'd been allowed to travel by herself because she was totally mad. I met her on the ship coming back from England in 1951 and I thought I'd do an experiment to find if you could manage without money. So I bought a ticket to Panama and left Sydney with sixpence, in 1953. I was twenty-four.

'While I was travelling with the nun we got free airfares, so she bought a cross and made me into a novice and dressed me up like her. We arrived at a hospital in Miami and it was all plate glass and chrome, and she asked for the Matron and said, "We are fellow travellers and we'd like to shelter here for the night." The Matron looked a bit taken aback but put us into a double maternity room, with our own little bathroom. I went into the bathroom and there was a big sign that said "If your water breaks dial 000." I've never had any children, I nearly fainted. Then I got into my waterproof bed next to the nun in her waterproof bed wearing her BVD underpants under her habit. And she snored so much there was no way I could go to sleep. I thought, this would have to be the dippiest night I'd ever had in my life.

'I left her eventually and then I started hitchhiking up the Federal Highway in Florida, where they rape you and chuck you to the alligators in the Everglades. The moment you got into any car there, they made a grab for your private area. And about the fifth car I got into I couldn't stand it any more and I just burst into tears and this marvellous Jewish American man, with sausage fingers and diamond rings all over them, said, 'Oh say, kid, you're in a bad way. Would you like to come home to my wife?' He was an ex-serviceman who'd married a maid at the Ritz Hotel who was a French Catholic. I stayed with them for quite a long time and went round to motels with a deck of cards telling fortunes.

'The ignominious end of this story is, I phoned Mother. The one terrible thing, though, is she sent me very little money because she didn't have a great deal, other than the fare back. I didn't really have anything to read except a Bible. I still think Ecclesiastes is marvellous.'

I wondered about her belief in God.

'Provided that God's not a male and provided that God is in plants and creatures. It's a very Buddhist sort of belief. I think death is probably the end of the show. You have such a build-up to life and learn so many beautiful things and experience such beautiful art and literature. It seems a most enormous waste, doesn't it? I think you probably go back into the pool of life force. But I don't think you have any personal identity any more.

As I was driving to her home I had noticed the name Cleland appears on the sign to the national nature reserve.

'It's a very Cleland district. My father's cousin, John, the park's called after him. Since 1925 he started lobbying the government to stop all the hills here being subdivided. There was a terrible building company called the Obelisk Building Company and they were going to cut the whole lot up. Fortunately, during the Depression they went bankrupt, so that went off. Then he kept lobbying the government, until in the 1940s, the government bought it all and then they got Warren Bonython to say how to make the best of the park. There are a lot of bullock tracks there, some of which were kept open. Warren made it so that the public couldn't get everywhere and wreck the whole place. But, on the other hand, they had nice access to it.'

Again there was this concern for sharing the good things with the rest of the community. No private retreats or walls or locked gates to keep the beauty solely for private family use.

'I worked in John Bray's law firm for seven years and then I came up here to live and work. I had a very good matrimonial practice here because people knew if you went into the Brookman Building in Grenfell Street you were going in to Jack Alderman's office for a divorce, whereas they could hide up here. Once the Family Court took over, it all became laborious and boring. It was lovely in the old Supreme Court, I never liked it much after that. But it used to be fun. Crazy things like some woman saying that her husband had a sexual penchant for vegetables, and we had to do the particulars of cruelty and she said he was always out in the vegetable garden doing dreadful sexual things to the vegetables. And we had to set this out in documents, so paragraph 13 on page 2 just said this: "Melon season was a nightmare."'

Did you know it is possible to laugh so much that champagne actually comes out of your nose?

Despite the hilarity and her making light of the sexual abuse she had suffered I kept coming back in my mind to the effects of the abuse and whether she had hated her uncle.

'I just thought he was a silly old fool. He didn't rape me. He was just a silly old fiddler. I thought it was all a bit distasteful and I felt so vulnerable, but there was nothing I could do about it. I did tell Mother eventually, when he was dead, and she said, "I'll kill him." And I said, "That's why I waited until he was dead because I knew you would." I didn't have any choice. The thing I hated most about him was he used to smoke cigarettes out of a holder that was never washed and it stank. The smell of that worried me more than what he was doing. It all stopped eventually.'

Had she ever confronted him?

'No.'

'Why not?'

'I think he might have died before I ever got the chance. He was very high up in the RSL. Very respected. Had photographs of himself shaking hands with the Queen. I don't think what happened to me is a very unique experience, I think it happened to a lot of people.'

I'm sure it did, but the way it scars them clearly has everything to do with the level of brutality of the actual abuse. Certainly not everyone who has been badly abused becomes a serial killer, but it seems no-one who has been sexually abused escapes unharmed.

On a lighter note, had she really appeared in court with nothing on but a fur coat?

'When I first got a job at Genters, Wilson and Bray, they paid me twenty pounds a week and I had a flat down on South Terrace that was seven guineas, and I only had two towels and two sets of clothing and a couple of sets of underwear. One day I didn't have anything clean and I did happen to have a mink coat. I had saved up for it. I thought, well, I'll just put some underclothing and my mink coat on. It was the middle of winter. I went into what was then the police court and they had the heating on full bore and I knew what it was like to be a polar bear at the Adelaide Zoo in the middle of summer. I had sweat running down my face. It was just dreadful.

'I think because I was brought up a strict Methodist I did go a bit to the other extreme. I shaved my pubes because I thought it was more hygienic. I only did that for a couple of years. I'd been to the Folies-Bergère and I thought they all looked pretty, shaved.

'When we had Nureyev [the legendary ballet dancer] here I had a little heated swimming pool over there and a lot of sheilas got in there naked with me. Nureyev came over, totally camp, of course, and he said to me, "See all those women? I'd like to whip them all." A bit like Prince Igor. And then he queried why I was shaven. I didn't bother to answer him. It was none of his business.'

I asked her why someone who loved to travel and had friends all over the world had never lived anywhere else.

'I've always loved Adelaide. It's compact, there're some interesting people to talk to, people leave you alone to do your own thing, there's a reasonable amount of fresh air and you can afford a reasonable chunk of real estate. It's got a lot of things going for it. I live a very isolated sort of life now but I'm really still reasonably happy. I don't eat in the evenings at all so I like seeing my friends in the lunch hour and there are a lot of good restaurants in the Hills, like The Bridgewater Mill. Privacy is important. I think back to Virginia Woolf, and *A Room of One's Own*. It's always been terribly important for our sex to be able to have somewhere they could do their own thing instead of being in rooms you have to share with children and dogs.

'It doesn't matter much where you are or what age you are or what sex you belong to or who you go to bed with, you creatively make your own life.'

~

Conversations with people like Pam are always salutary for baby boomers like me whose generation think they invented sex. And its revolution. Her creative spirit dates back to the wild-eyed radicals who left the repressions of the old country to live a free, sexually liberated life in the perfect colony, only to find the powerful Methodists and Presbyterians and Baptists had other ideas of exactly what constituted perfection. Just as the churches continue to sit side by side with the hotels in the city, the struggle for power between the religious and the radical forces is still part of the dynamic of the city. Almost everything in Pam's life was a reaction to the strength of her mother's Methodism.

She was determined to create her own Eden, her own Utopia, not only in terms of her physical surroundings but in her constant search for the best possible life, the best possible pleasure, the best possible fun. For her it was always midnight in the garden of good and evil. And it was only fun if you shared it with others. Seems fair.

III

PARADISE OF DISSENT

August 2003

THE NOVELIST Edna O'Brien branded August a wicked month and it was indeed wickedly cold when I returned again to Adelaide. Those in the village preferred the word 'bracing'. As the plane was landing at the airport, the captain's voice, warm and cheerful, buzzed over the intercom. 'Welcome to Adelaide, the temperature is currently 10 degrees.' The passengers, as one, emitted a groan. This was not right, they were affronted, this was Adelaide, meant to be the city with the Mediterranean climate. By the time we were all clattering down the rickety steel steps onto the tarmac, a light rain had started to fall.

I had foolishly been talked into leaving my winter overcoat in Sydney.

I called in to the courtroom to check out the two birds on the wire. Yes, there they were, still sitting in the dock in the same position as if carved in the same marble as the staircase. Nothing had changed. Everyone was in the same position, except for one juror who had left for personal reasons. The prosecutor was ploughing on with her evidence and her witnesses. Detail after meticulous detail. I retired to the bowels of the building and my scouring of the transcripts.

My focus was the young James Vlassakis, the Crown's chief witness, the teenage boy who had hero-worshipped John Bunting and asked him to be his father. Sexually abused and damaged, drug-addicted and encouraged to contribute to the murders by Bunting and Wagner, how did he feel when brought into the courts to give evidence against them and what did he feel about the victims he had helped to kill? This is what he said from the dock during the committal hearings.

I would like to begin by thanking Your Honour for giving me a chance to say how sorry I am to the people I've caused so much pain and suffering to. As I look back and reflect at the past, I wonder what went wrong and why I cannot change these terrible things I've done. If only I could change the past. I know that nothing I can ever say will justify the terrible way these people were viciously murdered, and no-one could ever deserve what had happened to them. I am myself sorry for the fact that I've done these degraded crimes. I have to live with the pain and suffering I've caused to the victims' families and friends. While I lie in bed at night I think I don't know myself any more and I try to come to terms with what I have done. In the mornings I wake up and think why? How could I do this? I have to live with this and when I look into the mirror and look at my face I think this is not me. How did I end up in this position? Those questions I can't answer but in time I hopefully can. I could kill myself tomorrow but then I think this would be the easy way out. Now I realise that the choices I've made are the ones that will affect my life forever. I can only hope by pleading guilty and giving evidence in the trial to come, I can offer a little peace to the families and friends of the victims by owning up to my mistakes and admitting my guilt to myself, society, relatives and friends.

~

On 4 April 1998 Vlassakis was living with Bunting, his mother, Elizabeth Harvey, who was in and out of psychiatric hospitals, his brothers and a drug-addicted drifter named Gavin Porter at 3 Burdekin Avenue in Murray Bridge. One night Vlassakis was disturbed from a drug-induced sleep haze by Bunting and told to accompany him to the back shed. Bunting took out a key and opened the door. He led him towards a barrel and lifted the lid. The pungent smell of rotting flesh attacked his nostrils.

'See that,' said Bunting, in a gloating voice, 'That's Barry's arse.'

Vlassakis couldn't see anything but an ugly mess of decomposing flesh.

'Michael's in there with him.'

When Vlassakis stepped back a foot or two to escape the stench he saw on the floor of the shed the body of Gavin Porter lying on his back with a rope around his neck. It was clear to him that Porter was dead.

Bunting kicked the dead body. He had always considered Porter a waste of oxygen.

'Stupid arsehole got the rope caught on his nose. Robert grabbed him from behind and started to strangle him and the bastard kept falling to his knees.' Here Bunting paused only to laugh aloud to himself as if he was sharing the biggest joke.

'I said, "Stand up straight you idiot, or we'll kill you."'

By now he was laughing so hard he was finding it difficult to stand up straight himself, but he imitated the way Porter had pulled himself up ramrod straight like a soldier on duty.

'Stupid bastard, died standing to attention.'

When he heard that arrogant laugh, all Vlassakis could think about was the fact that it was all true.

John hadn't been lying about killing Happy Pants. Once when they had been watching the television program *Australia's Most Wanted*, a segment had come on about a body found at Lower

Light. He remembered John having that same look in his eyes as he had tonight when he had claimed that the body was his artwork. When his mother had gone to bed, John had told Vlassakis how he had hit Happy Pants with a hammer, then gone down the road to get Barry and Robert to help him bury the body. They had taken it to Lower Light but the ground was so hard they could only dig a shallow grave.

'That was my work, all mine. I fixed him,' he kept repeating, with the same swaggering pride he was now displaying.

Vlassakis did his best to block out what he had seen that night in the shed by taking heroin and any amphetamines he could lay his hands on. Often when he was coming down from one of these drugs he would hear himself whimpering to Bunting about how his half-brother, Troy Youde, had sexually assaulted him and how much he hated him for it. Bunting would listen and sometimes he would tell James about his own abuse. These were the times when Bunting became most upset and would scream that Troy was 'a fucking waste' and that he would deal with him. He pledged his revenge. The more James sobbed, the more Bunting swore to get Troy back for what he had done.

On a cold morning in August 1998, only a bit over two months since he had seen the dead body of Gavin Porter, Vlassakis was again doped and asleep on the lounge when he was woken by Bunting and Wagner. Neither his mother nor his other brothers were home.

'Here, take these,' said Bunting, and tried to thrust a pair of handcuffs and a hunk of wood into his hands. Vlassakis stared hard at the wood and realised that it was the leg from his deceased grandmother's couch. He couldn't get his head around what was going on.

'Come on, wake up. Time we had a little talk with Troy Boy. Follow me and do as I say.'

With Bunting leading the way, they trooped into a bedroom where Troy was asleep on the floor. Bunting held up his hand and said, 'Now.' Wagner started hitting Troy. Bunting looked at James and, as directed, he hit Troy twice with the hunk of wood in his hand. Suddenly Troy jumped up and backed himself into the corner on top of the bed. That's when Bunting and Wagner took over, bashing him and shouting for him to get down.

'James, handcuff him,' yelled Bunting. 'Just cuff him. Now.'

Vlassakis grabbed the handcuffs and managed to get one on Troy's left arm and then stopped. He staggered out of the room while Bunting and Wagner secured the cuffs and dragged him towards the bathroom. Vlassakis was feeling sick but returned to the bathroom, where Troy was sitting in the bath, his hair matted with blood. He was screaming for them to let him go.

'Shut up. Just shut up, do as you're told and I'll let you go,' ordered Bunting in a quiet but authoritative voice at the same time he was trying to punch him in the testicles. Troy at first refused to open his legs but Bunting ripped off some toilet paper and told him to clean the blood off the sides of the bath. As soon as Troy attempted to do this and his legs opened, Bunting punched him hard between them. The more Troy screamed, the harder Wagner punched him in the chest and the head.

'Call me Lord Sir,' ordered Bunting. With Wagner's fist poised above his head, Troy stammered, 'Lord Sir.'

Bunting said, 'Now call Robert, God.'

Robert thumped him hard in the chest and when he had recovered enough breath Troy called him 'God.'

'What about James? What special name are you going to give James?' By this time Troy was crying and the more he cried, the more Wagner hit him.

'Name him. Name your brother that you molested, you dirty. Make it good.'

Troy muttered, 'Moses.'

'That's a Jew's name, stupid.'

Wagner shouted, 'We don't want no Jews here,' and punched him hard in the chest.

'Let me speak,' pleaded Troy.

'Use his name,' threatened Wagner.

'Let me speak, Lord Sir, please let me speak.'

'Shut up. You're a dirty. You're a waste of oxygen.'

'Please,' Troy looked to Robert.

'Please who?' shouted Bunting.

'Please God.'

'Shut your mouth. Speak when you're spoken to.'

Bunting turned to Vlassakis and told him to get a bag from the table in the lounge room. Wagner seized pliers from the bag that James handed him and proceeded to squeeze Troy's toes and then his toenails. When Troy screamed louder at the squeezing of the nails, Wagner laughed and said to James, 'Now you know the difference.'

After Wagner had demonstrated this several times, Bunting grabbed the tape recorder, turned it on and ordered Troy to say he was going to Perth, to abuse his mother and then his brothers. Then he demanded to know his PIN number. Troy was sobbing as he told him.

Wagner kept laughing and mocking his voice, shrieking, 'Mummy, Mummy, I want my mummy,' then he stuffed a gag in his mouth and continued to hit him.

'Tie the rope around his neck,' ordered Bunting. Robert did as he was told and, using a car jack handle, Bunting started to twist the rope.

'I could do this all day,' he joked to Wagner, 'this is fun.' Robert was laughing along with Bunting and then Bunting let him take his turn twisting the rope.

Vlassakis was lurking out in the hallway when Bunting

grabbed him and said, 'Come and make him apologise to you for what he did.'

'He already has, John.'

'Make him do it now. Now. This is revenge time.'

Vlassakis knelt down by the side of the bath where Troy was lying in a shallow sea of blood, half-conscious. Wagner slackened his grip while James told him to apologise. Troy said he already had, he was sorry for what he'd done.

Bunting, not satisfied with this, knelt down beside James, and said to Troy, 'I've got you all. One by one. Taken you to the clinic. This is what you deserve. This is the only way to cure you. I've already cured Michael and Barry and Ray and Gavin and Happy Pants . . . Have I forgotten any?'

Wagner laughed heartily and said, 'I don't think you've forgotten anyone.' And then with his big, strong hands he twisted the rope very hard while Bunting looked into Troy's eyes eager for the signs of death. When he was sure that Troy was dead, he turned to James and said, 'Now kick him in the head.'

When James hesitated, he said: 'Do it. This is your last chance before your mother comes home.'

Vlassakis closed his eyes and kicked, hitting the bathtub. Bunting and Wagner laughed and cheered.

Bunting sent Vlassakis to Woolworths at Murray Bridge to buy some strong rubbish bags and boxes of gloves. When he returned, Troy had been taken out of the bath and was lying on the floor, his feet pointing towards the door. Bunting said, 'We'd better make sure he's really dead,' and nodded at Wagner, who stood on Troy's chest. The air from Troy's lungs burst out of his nose, making a grunting, farting noise, which Bunting and Wagner thought was so hilarious that Wagner did it again.

Bunting wrapped Troy's body in the rubbish bags, taping them around his head and torso, and then tied his legs together. They carried his body into the shed, placing it just inside the door. Bunting locked the shed and they all followed him inside. Vlassakis said he needed some methadone and when he returned, doped, from the chemist, Bunting announced he was hungry and insisted they all go to McDonald's. Vlassakis didn't eat much but the others had hearty appetites.

When Elizabeth Harvey returned to the house that afternoon, Bunting told her that James and Troy had been involved in a big fight and that Troy had left. She was very upset and went into his room to check his belongings. They were, of course, gone. That night Bunting and Vlassakis drove to a nearby hardware store and bought a plastic barrel. This was placed in the shed, Bunting locking the door behind them. Bunting pulled on some gloves and they hauled Troy head-first into the barrel.

'This will have to be a "slice and dice",' announced Bunting in a loud voice and proceeded to expertly cut off Troy's foot at the ankle. While he was cutting through the tendons and the muscle and slicing in a circular motion around the bone, he explained in professional tones to James exactly what he was doing and why. Having placed Troy's foot on the edge of the barrel he demonstrated by snapping it out of its socket, flinging it into the barrel and moving the barrel next to the other two. Having absolutely no sense of smell, he lifted the lid on the barrel where he had placed Gavin Porter and asked James, 'What's the smell like?'

When James told him it was bad, very bad, Bunting looked very pleased with himself, displayed his special gloating smile and said, 'He's rotting nicely, then.' He did the same with the other barrel and replied in exactly the same words. His self-constructed rituals were followed with the same solemnity as a priest performing a Mass.

After Bunting had locked the shed, he handed Vlassakis Troy's ATM card and the PIN number.

'He owes you this for what he done to you. Use it wisely.'

Vlassakis used the money in Troy's account to buy amphetamines and petrol.

~

The State Opera of South Australia was performing a specially commissioned work titled *Dead Man Walking*. Now, you may think that an opera about a murderer on death row would be the last production I would want to see but, in fact, I was drawn to it precisely because of the many comments I had heard from normally mild-mannered people who told me that in the case of serial killers or terrorists, we should reintroduce the death penalty. Even the prime minister had said in the media that perhaps it was time to revisit the debate. Christopher Pearson had written a column in the *Australian* in favour of its reintroduction for 'crimes against humanity'. I totally disagreed with him. There were, however, many who disagreed with me. Talkback radio was dominated by debates over how we should deal with the Bali bombers, who had not only shown no respect for human life but celebrated their acts of terrorism. Like Hitler and Stalin, terrorists lack all empathy for their victims, blinded as they are by irrational emotions. Vigilantes are a species of domestic terrorist.

I could not help thinking about Bunting and Wagner's zealotry, about their absolute belief in their right to kill those they considered had ruined the lives of children, as their lives had been ruined. Like terrorists, they revelled in the pain of their victims. They celebrated their murders. If the death penalty were still in force in South Australia I was sure that they would be facing it.

I do understand how individuals who have had one of their own cruelly taken from them desire revenge. Why should murderers be allowed to live, they argue, when their innocent victims have no life at all? It is a perfectly understandable reaction. Grief and anger swamp rational thought and reasoned argument. And if the victim was someone I loved, I could not be sure that my desire for revenge would not be as overwhelming. It is, however, I believe, crucial to our future as a civilised country that people who are in favour of the reintroduction of the death penalty understand why such a move would diminish us as human beings and weaken our sense of ourselves and what we stand for. There is, in my view, a huge difference between the individual desire for capital punishment and the communal reasons we should never go back to enshrining such emotions in law. No matter what the circumstances.

As human beings we bob back and forth between good and evil all our lives. Most of us, fortunately, never cross the threshold into savagery. As civilised people we hold to a collective central belief in the value and dignity of all human life. No-one in Australia – and that includes those representing the state – has by law the right to take a life. I think once we lose that centre, that core belief, which has taken us so long to reach, we lose the right to think of ourselves as a civilised people. A sense of moral righteousness does not justify violence.

I am sure that Bunting and Wagner had both convinced themselves that they were somehow doing the state's work for them by ridding the world of paedophiles. They probably believed they were performing a community service. This is always the vigilante's justification. Such, however, was their rage and their hurt and their damage, that they could not prevent their slide into torture and savagery as well as murder. Once they had given in to their basest instincts, there were no limits to what they were capable of doing to their victims.

These were my preoccupations as I entered the theatre. Sister Helen Prejean, on whose book the opera was based, had attended its opening night in Adelaide and been involved in public discussions on the issues. From its earliest beginnings

Adelaide had been called a 'paradise of dissent' because so many of its founders were involved in the intellectual issues of their day, focusing always on the best and fairest means of organising and running a society. There were Chartists and prison reformers, teetotallers and suffragists. In fact, every kind of radical dissenting thinker was among the early settlers. Such people are attracted, no doubt, to the whole notion of building a Utopia. It was no accident that South Australia was not only the first state in the country to grant women the right to vote but the second in the world to grant female suffrage, only pipped by New Zealand, who is still ahead of us in electing a female prime minister. South Australia was, however, in 1894 the first in the world to grant women the right to stand for election to parliament. Radical ideas of both the left and the right have always been topics of discussion in Adelaide and every year now in 'The Festival State', as the car numberplates proclaim, there is also a Festival of Ideas.

It was no surprise to me that there was a full house in the theatre and that Adelaide was hosting the Australian premiere of this controversial opera, commissioned and first performed in San Francisco. The facts are that, in 1985, Sister Helen Prejean accompanied convicted murderer Patrick Sonnier to his death. He was executed at the Angola State Penitentiary in Louisiana in the presence of the murder victim's family.

The opera opens with the murder itself. He is clearly guilty and yet seemingly remorseless about his crime. I was, of course, thinking not so much about him but about the unemotional faces that were fixed in my mind – Bunting and Wagner, sitting every day in the Adelaide law courts.

The opera concludes with Sister Helen's love for this flawed human being becoming the catalyst for his admission of guilt and his plea for forgiveness from the victim's family. Sister Helen has Christ's compassion for a man who is not only a murderer but a human being who is tortured and suffering. It does not stop the state taking his life.

It was an emotional and moving experience as a piece of theatre but I knew that by the last curtain call, everyone in the audience was asking themselves the question: do we, as the state, have the right to take someone's life?

I was asking myself how this story would be different had the murderer not admitted he was wrong and had he never shown compassion for his victims and their families. What if the murderer is judged to be incapable of such feelings? What if the murderer is a psychopath?

What exactly is a psychopath?

~

My first task the next day was not only to pay my usual visit to the accused murderers in the court but to find the transcript of the psychiatrist's evidence to the jury. The barristers defending Bunting and Wagner had not attempted from a psychiatric viewpoint to explain or analyse their behaviour. No doubt the police had asked for psychiatric reports but they were suppressed until the end, not just of this trial, but of Mark Haydon's which was due to follow in 2004.

Bunting and Wagner were enough for me to be trying to understand.

Evidence was given to the court on behalf of the Crown by Professor Mullins, who has extensive qualifications in analysing similar cases of serial killing. He has given evidence before courts in Britain, New Zealand and other states in Australia.

Let me quote from what he said to the court:

> Serial killings involving more than one person as a perpetrator are extremely rare. Bunting had become totally preoccupied, if the accounts are right, with the notion of a conspiracy of

paedophiles, a network of paedophiles and preoccupied with the notion that somehow he had a role to save and protect children. First of all in the early stages, according to Vlassakis, by exposing paedophiles, later by killing them. He appears to have been constantly preoccupied with these themes and to have drawn others into his preoccupations . . .

By and large the people who perpetrate serial killings, at least within our sorts of societies, are people driven by perverse sexual motivations. On the face of it, the possibility is that this man is profoundly disturbed in this area and the question is why and how he's come to be totally preoccupied and used that preoccupation to justify the most horrific of acts. I'm not for a moment suggesting that you can explain these crimes by Mr Bunting's preoccupation with paedophiles and the dangers they present. Clearly there are other elements that came into this dreadful mixture, which led to these crimes but these provide . . . the superficial justification for his actions, the way he justified himself to others and probably the way he justified himself to himself.

To explain those actions one needs to look for other forces than simply a set of odd and extraordinary beliefs about the danger presented by paedophiles. Even in themselves the accounts and the material raise very real questions over . . . how this man came to be so preoccupied and so forceful that he was able to carry others along with him . . .

You can be both psychopathic and psychotic. The two are not incompatible. On the material available you wonder whether Bunting might not partake of both forms of disturbance . . . There are some particularly unusual features with respect to this case, particularly with respect to the retention of the bodies. Vlassakis, who insisted he had no part, and I think there are reasons to accept he had no part, in the retention of these bodies, is not in a position to explain why they were retained. The keeping of trophies, bodies or mementos are features seen in serial killings in psychiatric terms.

Both the accused would, no doubt, scoff at the psychiatrist's analysis of their behaviour. They would be the first to deny that they were mentally sick. In their minds, their mission was to rid the world of the sexually and mentally sick. No mention of their mental condition had been made by their defence counsel. Nor was the psychiatrist asked to assess them. Clearly the defence counsel did not want to explore those areas.

~

Over the course of 1998, Bunting and Wagner embarked on a killing spree that seemed to gather momentum with each new murder. They moved from one to the next in a kind of zealous frenzy. With Gavin Porter and Troy Youde decomposing in barrels in the shed at 3 Burdekin Avenue, Fred Brooks was the next victim to be killed there.

This is Vlassakis's account as he told it to the jury of what happened. This is the monologue of a murder and a murderer. Remember that Vlassakis loved John Bunting, that he was the father he'd never had, the father who promised to protect him, the father who took him for rides on his BMW motorbike, who showed him his collection of guns, who attempted to desensitise him by teaching him to shoot dogs and cats and skin them. Vlassakis began by hero-worshipping Bunting, wanting to emulate him, desiring his approval and then fearing his punishment.

Bunting told me that Fred Brooks was a dirty. He said he was supposed to be touching up little girls and he needed to go to the clinic. He repeated it hundreds of times in the car, at home at 3 Burdekin Avenue, whenever we were together. They were the disease, he was the cure. They had to go to the clinic to be cured, to make them good. If a person needed to go to the clinic it meant they needed to be killed.

He asked me to meet Fred Brooks and see what I thought of him, if he was a dirty or not. I just thought he was very slow, he had learning difficulties and I said he quite possibly could have been one but he was very young, only around seventeen. Bunting just kept talking about the allegations with a little girl. He told Fred they were going to steal some computers and they were both playing with the handcuffs. Fred had taken them off and then Robert Wagner put the thumbcuffs on him, grabbed Fred from behind. He started to choke him. Fred started to try and move. He was falling down and Robert picked him up. John had moved into the front of Fred and he was talking very loudly, not quite yelling at Robert to let him go.

'You're going to kill him, let him get some air.' Robert let him go a little bit so he could get a breath and told Fred to behave himself, to be good. Not to kick, not to scream. He said, 'If you hurt us we will hurt you.'

I'd started to walk down the hallway, had turned around and saw John and Robert pulling him into the bathroom. He was told to sit in the bath. He tried to get out of the handcuffs in the bath and John told him to stop and hit him. After Robert had grabbed him Bunting was very serious, very direct. Fred's T-shirt was taken off, then his jeans and he was sitting in the bath in his jocks. John Bunting then told him he had to be good again and then there were a few hits and punches in the balls from John and Robert.

Then the tape recorder was produced. John asked Fred about touching a little girl. Fred denied it. Then the Variac was produced. He said, 'This is a Variac machine, it goes from zero to 260 volts.'

The Variac machine looks similar to a car alternator, but with a big dial on the top. The machine was black, with a lead that would go into the wall to the power point. Bunting clipped the clamps onto his balls and his penis. He asked him again about the little girl and he denied it so then turned on the machine and put it up to twenty volts. Fred started kicking in the bath and John turned it down pretty much straight away. John then asked him again and Fred said, 'Yes, I did it.' After that I was told to hit him. I hit him with the bottom of my hand, it wasn't a fully closed fist, about four times.

Robert and myself were smoking and there was no ashtray and I said, 'What do I use for an ashtray?' And John said, 'Just use the dirty.' I can't remember what cigarette John grabbed, if it was mine or Robert's, but he stuck it up Fred Brooks' nose. Then he grabbed another cigarette butt, still lit, and put it in Fred's right ear. He was blowing on the cigarette to keep it alight and it was burning his ear. Robert had grabbed his cigarette lighter and started to heat the lighter up. He said, 'I'm going to give him a smiley.' After the cigarette lighter had been heated up, he put the lighter on his forehead and started to burn Fred. Fred had moved and Robert said that he had spoilt it. Then he started to burn Fred's nipple with the lighter. The skin went really white and there was a terrible smell. Then the tape recorder was produced and he got Fred to repeat phrases. Fred was asked his PIN numbers, his bank accounts, etc. When Bunting was asking Fred the questions his tone was very direct, slightly angry, very hard to explain. The Variac machine was used twice and then finally when he said yes.

After the tape recording was made and all the questions had been asked, Fred had his jocks taken off. Robert fumbled into the plastic bag and got out a box of sparklers and a pair of pliers. There was some toenail squishing with the pliers then they grabbed the box of sparklers, used the pliers to cut off the part you held it with and John put the sparkler into the eye of Fred's penis and then lit the sparkler. As it was burning down Fred was moving because it was burning him. It burned down all the way. They did it again after that. Then Robert grabbed Fred Brooks' penis and started to twist it up and then used his hand to hit the top of his penis.

Some time after that John grabbed the jack handle, which was in the bathroom, and started hitting Fred across his arm and shoulder blade. I'd never seen John lose it the way he did. He just kept hitting Fred with the jack handle. His arm had broken, the shoulder had gone all purple. I'm not sure if Fred Brooks had been gagged before that happened or just after.

Then there was a box of syringes in the bathroom. Robert and John filled the syringes up with water and then injected Fred in the balls with a syringe full of water. They did that several times. I was standing next to the door watching. He was gagged with a sock and tape. After cleaning up, John wrapped Fred in plastic garbage bags and put him in the boot of the Torana.

I can't remember how he was finally murdered but right at the end John told Fred he'd done this before and listed off the names of the people he'd murdered, exactly the same way as he had done in Troy's murder. Just after Fred Brooks was put in the bath and the tape recordings were made, John told me to put on the CD by the band Live, the album was called *Throwing Copper*. He told me to put it on track two. The lyrics went, 'we will not be bashed, raped or scarred.'

It was used in all the murders I was there for. He also told Fred to call him 'Lord Sir', to call Robert 'God' and he said he wasn't happy with the name 'Master' that Troy had given me, he wanted Fred Brooks to rename me. Fred said a few names but ended up saying Master, which was the same. He called Robert and John by those names but he didn't speak to me. When John had grabbed the jack handle and hit Fred, I got scared because I'd never seen John lose his temper quite like that. He just kept hitting and hitting and hitting. And hitting.

~

Not long after the murder of Fred Brooks, Bunting told Vlassakis that he was sleeping with Jodie Elliott, Fred's mother. She had arrived from Queensland in mid-1998 and she and her son began living with her sister, Elizabeth Haydon, and her husband, Mark Haydon, at Catalina Road, Elizabeth. When Jodie's son went missing Bunting told her that he had run away and didn't want anything more to do with her. When she telephoned Fred's mobile, all she received were abusive messages. Bunting told Vlassakis that he was only sleeping with her to keep her quiet and to use her. Jodie told Bunting she was concerned about her son's disappearance because he had an ATM card and they had a joint account. A few days later Bunting gave Jodie the ATM card, saying he'd found it on the doorstep. He told her that Fred was suffering from schizophrenia and staying with friends, and that when he was better he'd ring her but until then she should leave him alone. Jodie believed him because she also believed she and Bunting had become engaged. She had even set a wedding date, until he eventually told her that the wedding could not go ahead because he wasn't divorced from his wife, V.

~

The position of Lord Mayor of Adelaide is an elected office, voted on from within the closed circle of city councillors. It is a powerful position, fraught with conflicting vested interests, particularly from the business sector of the city. Not overtly political in the sense that no party label or support is displayed, it is nevertheless a pathway to political office because of its high public and media profile. Jane Lomax-Smith, a London doctor, had come to Adelaide in the 1970s with her Adelaide-born lawyer husband, Tim Woolley. She liked the radical ideas of the Labor government led by the charismatic premier Don Dunstan and decided to make Adelaide her home. She became lord mayor in the late 1990s and was subsequently recruited into the Labor Party, winning the high-profile battle for the seat of Adelaide against one of her former councillors, the Liberal Party candidate Michael Harbison, who went on to become the current lord mayor. They are diametrically opposed and typify the ongoing battle of dissenting ideas that is so much a part of the city's character.

Jane, who is on the left of her party, lives in a very unpretentious cottage in the western end of the city with her husband, who is a lawyer for the Aboriginal Legal Rights Movement, her two school-age sons, and several chooks that wander freely about the cottage's back courtyard. Michael is on the right of the Liberal Party, lives in a stone mansion in the Establishment suburb of Medindie with his wife and three children. He has no chooks.

Jane comes from a London working-class background. Michael went to the prestigious St Peter's boys' college and his father was a country doctor.

Their fights on the city council were legendary and their battle over the seat of Adelaide was watched closely and enthusiastically by the citizens of Adelaide, as it resembled something between a soap opera and a blood sport.

Now the Minister of Tourism, Education and Youth Employment, Jane met me for coffee at the Three Benches in Dulwich, where we sat outside soaking up the winter sunshine. She is tall, lean, fit from jogging every day and has a high-cheekboned

Jamie Lee Curtis look. There's an energy, intellectual and physical, about her which I was pleased to see political office had not destroyed.

As she had a school function to attend later in the morning I jumped straight in with a question about the Snowtown murders and how damaging she thought the publicity was as the Minister for Tourism, especially given the tourism campaign is based on the theme of 'Secrets'.

What about the London tabloid that had named Adelaide 'the murder capital of the world'?

'I think that it was grossly unfair, especially when you think of the rates of murder in Johannesburg, Moscow, Paris. I mean, London is singularly dangerous and the statistics about the likelihood of being a victim of crime in those countries, and even any other country of the world, is so high. Such sloppy journalism.

'There is a percentage of aberrant, deviant behaviour that's probably fixed in all communities. But in larger cities it's masked by a much larger percentage of random violence, break and enters, drug-related crimes, and you don't notice it. My theory is that we're looking, if you like, at the sediment at the bottom of a river and because the river's dried out you can see the sediment. That's why it appears that in small places you often get unusual crimes. They happen everywhere but are masked by the multiplicity of all the other crimes.

'As for the tourism campaign based around the word 'Secrets', I don't think it has been damaged or impacted on, because we still attract very large numbers of interstate visitors and it's a brand that's been around for a long time. I don't think people who live here sense that there are weird murders in our community. The percentage is so minuscule. The media in the UK related the Snowtown murders to the Falconio murder in the Northern Territory, so you compound sloppy journalism with a lack of geographical knowledge and not even a hint of the facts and you get tabloid hysteria. I also make the point repeatedly that the poms are used to tacky journalism in their newspapers, and so they would see that and laugh because just about every pom has a relative, a friend here, or has visited Australia, and they know how safe it is. It's hard to imagine that the image of Adelaide will be impacted by such a piece of appalling journalism. I mean, when you've lived in London and you've heard of people being shot for their mobile phones and you know the incidence of rape and murder in your own streets, you're hardly impressed by that kind of journalism.

'In my experience, Adelaide isn't a closed enclave either, because I'm foreign and an outsider who wasn't an Australian citizen until 1990 and I was elected lord mayor by 1997. That doesn't smack of a closed, unwelcoming community. That speaks of something different to me.

'When I first arrived here it was vibrant and exciting and different. The story I'd been told when I was offered the job at Adelaide University was along the lines of, "You probably wouldn't like Australia, it's a terrible redneck place but Adelaide's different. It's the renaissance capital of the southern hemisphere." That sort of feeling was apparent then because it was vibrant and it was regarded as a magnet for talent rather than a town that everyone left. They were the Dunstan years. I hope there'll be more of that in the next twenty years. It's like all cycles of politics and culture, they come and they go and they change things irrevocably. I think that in terms of ideas we are still world-class.

'My Adelaide is probably slightly quirky because, after all, I am a foreigner, even though I'm an Australian citizen. I see things differently and I'm always surprised that I still find things that catch me out. The thing that shocks me most is that people moan so much. They don't realise how lucky they are. That's because of the isolation.

'Law and order is a growth industry across the whole of Australia. And it's partly to do with people's perceptions of crime rates as well, because people have a perception that life is very dangerous. In fact, it's actually quite safe.

'My areas of intimacy within the city are quite narrow. Curiously, just about everywhere I've lived is in the state seat of Adelaide, because I live in the city and I've briefly lived in North Adelaide, Prospect, Walkerville. Everywhere I've lived is within walking distance of each other, and when the children were small I had one of those old-fashioned prams and I would walk everywhere, which is, I think, one of Adelaide's charms.

'Adelaide's strengths are a combination of the arts, the academic and the gastronomic. Clearly, a city would not be sustainable if you couldn't nurture yourself through the performance of music and other activities, like the Festival of Ideas and Writers' Week. I have no interest in cooking but I find the idea of writing about food interesting as a cultural and geographical and sociological process, and what the food writers did at Tasting Australia is just astounding because it is like Writers' Week at the Adelaide Festival. We've also got the Central Market. It's so easy to drive in and park. It's not just the fact that the produce is here, in terms of being able to get everything from goat's cheese to good olives and all the fish and every ingredient you could possibly want. The science and technology of food is well displayed, whether it's in knowledge or research or food science research. It's just part of the culture and it's part of the landscape and it belongs here. It's not as if someone has come in and said, "Oh, we'll make it a food capital, it's got all the ingredients." It was all here from the beginning. When I talk to people from overseas I always say, "Seven per cent of the population, 70 per cent of the fine wine, it can't be bad." It's a great statistic.

'Honestly, if we can't get it right, then no-one can. I often think Adelaide's the last chance for civilisation. Sydney is on the downhill path. It has no hope with its water supply, its air pollution, its environmental standards. Whereas Adelaide still has a chance to get its environment together. It still has the chance to be a viable community. It still has the chance to collaborate and have people talking together and doing things differently. There is still a chance that because of its size we can actually work together to solve the same problems that beset every city in the western world.

'If you look at a problem like homelessness or inadequate housing, it's not just about building houses. It's about mental health. It's about employment. It's about education. It's about literacy. You have to actually get a collaboration between the players to solve the problem.'

Then, as is the lot of politicians, she had to leave as quickly as she had arrived. There was another group of people awaiting her attention.

~

I visited her nemesis, Lord Mayor Michael Harbison, at the Town Hall, noting the portrait of Colonel Light as I was ushered down the long passage to the mayoral chambers. A huge room full of antique furniture, panelled wood and old leather chairs greeted me. Only the stench of stale cigar smoke was missing. At first glance Michael looks just like any other businessman in his white shirt, striped tie and grey business suit, but not too many lord mayors started their career in the circus.

What excited him enough about Adelaide to want to be its lord mayor? Why, as a rich and successful businessman, does he choose to remain here when he could live anywhere in the world?

'I think it's a city whose time has come. It's an ideal city, one of the most successful cities of the twenty-first century.'

I wondered whether it was dangerous even to use words such as 'ideal'. Such concepts leave no place for flaws, let alone working out how to deal with them. On the other hand, if you don't have ideals, you have no idea of what you are striving for, what you are trying to achieve. It's the perennial Adelaide contradiction.

'Until recently Adelaide suffered from isolation but because of the worldwide computer networks we have, that's no longer an issue. Whether it's going to succeed as a city of the future depends upon the qualities of its design in terms of what is to become the economic activity of the future. That lies in the knowledge industry, and for the knowledge industry, you need a city which is both livable, culturally vibrant and which actually works. What Colonel Light designed in the late Georgian period is a city based on this dense but permeable grid and it all comes from the utilitarian movement where you have a city that, by its shape and its design, facilitates and governs people's behaviour. For example, it has wide, straight streets, so that there is unlikely to be bad behaviour because it would be probable that it would be observed and so on. That's the theory . . . In the square mile of the square grid in the centre, we could have 50,000 people living, 150,000 people working and 75,000 students studying and something like 150,000 people visiting each day. That would be its absolute peak and what I'm trying to do in this decade that I'm steering the city is to push us as far along on that continuum as we possibly can, using the central design of the city.

'The growth industries of tomorrow are the knowledge industries. In the old days you tended to have to do the knowledge work on-site. So, if you were a pathologist you sat in the corner of a hospital and someone brought in your samples in buckets. You put them under the microscope slide and you'd do your analysis of them. Then you'd write down the answer: this person has cancer or they don't. And you'd walk down the corridor and give it to the nurse on the ward. In the modern world, with computer networks and so on, you actually get your data coming in down the line and you do your data analysis on computer, you type in your answers, your diagnosis and you punch it out by email.'

'How fascinating,' I say, 'that you have chosen a pathologist as an example. Is that a Freudian slip? That's Jane Lomax-Smith's profession. Why do you think she beat you in the election?'

He shifts uncomfortably in his vast leather chair, pauses, smiles and then answers like a true politician.

'She was a stellar candidate. This is the job that I really want. That attempt to win the seat of Adelaide was a bit of a sideshow. I gave it my best shot but I'm not unhappy.'

'Is it your next goal?'

'No, it isn't my next goal. This is what I want to do, create a city of the future. After that, I'll go fishing.'

'Sure, Michael . . . but I'll leave that for later. Let's get back to Adelaide.'

'It was very exciting in the 1970s when I was growing up. But it has some qualities which I love dearly that are not just about the fact that I grew up here. It has this terrific ability for us all to communicate with each other and do things together when we want to. It starts with the design and scale of the city. You can walk to everything. Charles Landry, this fellow who was brought out by the government as part of its Thinker in Residence program, said that what you've got to do is make Adelaide a creative city. We met sitting at café tables in the East End where I work and I discovered that what he was talking about was the life that I was living. The reason I could do business so successfully there was the way the city worked because eventually everyone walked past my café table. I could meet, at some time of the day, anyone in the city, from the premier to the mayor or other businesspeople, simply by sitting at the café tables in the East End.

'The task was to make the rest of the city like this. It's not about skyscrapers and an Oklahoma City approach to the world, but rather it's about that kind of slightly gritty, grotty, creative mix. That's given me this notion about what a modern city really is like, which is having that kind of very dense, exciting mixture where you live, learn, work and play, all in the same spot. When I owned the magazine *City Limits* in London and I was commuting there, the kids in the London office all used to disappear to Berlin for the weekend. I've always believed in that saying, "When a man's tired of London he's tired of life," but they said to me, "Berlin is more exciting." When I got there I saw that it was true, and yet East Berlin was 500 miles from anywhere. This was before the Berlin Wall came down. There was no money and just a stock of old, tottery buildings and yet all the kids from London wanted to be there all the time. It was the most exciting city. Restricted by lack of capital and no development of buildings, they had put everything into all of these Victorian buildings, so you would have on the ground-floor cafés and retail, the first and second floor would be offices, where they all worked, and then the next two or three storeys were where they lived in apartments. That gave it this terrifically vibrant ambience. I'm not sure that it's still there now that the wall has come down and money has arrived, but I've seen it again recently in Dublin where you get that terrific street life.

'After I left school at St Peter's College, I went to Flinders University and studied Drama and Philosophy and Psychology and became very interested in popular theatre, in particular, the circus. I asked myself this question: what is a contemporary circus? I figured that when it was successful, it probably brought together the leading edge of many different art forms. Toulouse-Lautrec did his most innovative work doing circus posters. I figured that what I needed to do first was to work in the traditional circuses and learn the skills that I would need to bring into this contemporary circus which I was going to create.

'So I left university and joined Ashton's Circus as a tent-hand but I kept in touch with my mates in modern dance, drama and film. I learned to put up tents and be a tent boss, do business and advance bookings for circuses and finally became ringmaster for Ashton's Circus and later ringmaster for Circus Royale. I also went to see the film *Les Enfants du Paradis* one night, with Jean-Louis Barrault and it really moved me. I knew then that I had to stop preparing and just start. The Royal Adelaide Show was on the next day, so I said to my mates, "Let's start." We hid our unicycles under our greatcoats and smuggled them all into the Royal Show and did this performance. It was amazing because there were hundreds of people watching and we must have collected a hundred dollars in the hat, which was big money back in 1973. In those days no-one had ever seen a modern clown or a sword-swallower. I did fire-eating. But we all used to do everything.

'After a few hours the security guys at the show arrested us and kicked us out. Next morning, on the front page of the *Advertiser* there was a picture of me blowing fire. No-one had ever seen a fire-eater in Australia before. Somehow the director of the Royal Show found out where I was living, just around here near Gillies Street, and knocked on the door, a terribly polite, very distinguished gentleman with this grotty bunch of hippies living in a squat and he said: "Mr Harbison, I'd like to apologise for having you thrown out of the show yesterday. We would be very grateful if you would come back." So we did and had this most amazing season, made an enormous amount of money passing the hat and it grew like wildfire from there.

'The show got bigger and I started to feel I had proved what contemporary circus was and could be. To me it was an intellectual exercise, running this cooperative of thirty or forty people where basically we'd divvy up [the money] and get about sixty bucks a week each. It was pretty hard work. Finally, I said to the gang: "I've proved everything I want to prove, it's a wonderful thing but I want my life back. I want to go into business and make some money so I've got the freedom to do the things I want to do."

'In the circus, what's necessary is always possible. I learnt a lot in my circus days but I've always been very good at doing whatever it took to achieve whatever had to be done. A mate of mine wanted to buy a motorbike shop; we found one for two thousand dollars. He only had a thousand so I said, "Okay, I'll give you a thousand, we'll buy half each." I sold my half, a year later for $30,000. In the next year I used that to start renovating houses. I had two teams of workmen and I would buy a stone house a week, renovate them, rent them out and reset the finance. Theoretically, some cash was supposed to come out but it never did. After twelve months, on paper, we were worth a million bucks. One day my partner in that, Tim Hartley, came in and said, "Mick, I've got a big one." It was thirty-five houses and there was this funny, old-fashioned lemonade company as well. The Woodroofe family accepted the offer of one and a half million. Basically, we financed it on Bankcard, because we didn't have a lot of cash.

'After about four years I was getting really worn out, and we had this group of advisers and I managed to talk them into the idea that we float the business on the stock exchange. It was the first float that had been done for years in Adelaide, ever since Poseidon. We floated the thing for about $8 million and that enabled us to hire a managing director and left me free to do other things. So we did a few corporate raids on other companies. We bought 10 per cent of Simpsons and went down to them and said why don't you appoint me managing director. They laughed at us. So we sold the 10 per cent to E-mail and they got taken over.

'Our office was in the southern end of the lemonade factory and it was freezing. Tim and I just decided we couldn't stand another winter without sun so we wrote out the specs for our next acquisition. It had to have a northerly aspect, be in the centre of the city where it was fun. That's how we found Malcolm Reid, an old Adelaide furniture business, and set about building up the biggest furniture business in Australia, which we did in eighteen months. We sold Woodies Lemonade Company to the SA Brewing Company. Eventually we sold a lot of the furniture stores to their managers and when the bottom fell out of the stock market we bought back all our public companies, privatised them and decided we'd retire.

'We took our families around the world for about a year, returned to Adelaide, and I started to look for another business. I figured that information was what the 1990s would be all about so I looked for an information business that had access to a bigger market. I went to London to try to buy the magazine *Punch*, and, in fact, offered Pearsons $10 million for the *Punch* name but they wouldn't sell it. Instead, I bought *City Limits*. Unfortunately, three months after my offer Pearsons gave up on *Punch* and closed it, which was a bit of a shame because I would have had such fun with it.

'I struggled with *City Limits* for about a year but commuting monthly to London was a nightmare. My wife wouldn't leave Adelaide because she loves it. When the Internet happened I discovered that I didn't have to be culturally isolated from the rest of the world and, in fact, here in the East End, where I still owned all of this property, I could create this new renaissance city that would be like Berlin but connected to the rest of the world. That culminated in the multimedia syndicate of Microsoft, Telstra and the universities. Eventually I had the notion that what I really needed to do was to create that in the whole city and so I said, "I'll run for Council. If I'm elected,

I'll quit all of my business work." So that's why I'm here, to bring all of my talents together to make this a creative city.'

Here I was back in the land of Utopian dreams, with a twenty-first century Adelaide man using his energy and his creativity to plan the perfect city.

The perfect city indeed. Such notions were in his cultural DNA. He was a modern version of all the men that had first planned the city, a successful modern businessman with a Renaissance sensibility. But what was the cost of the notion of perfection? An ignorance of what lay outside the planned Utopia?

'Would you like to stay and have drinks with members of the High Court?' asked Michael. 'They're in Adelaide for a conference.'

'Thank you for the invitation but I think I'll pass. I'm a bit full up with murder and the law at the moment.'

He smiled and his young PR assistant showed me to the huge oak-panelled door.

I waved goodbye to Colonel Light on my way out of the Town Hall foyer. 'See you later, William. You have no idea what you started.'

～

A mere forty-minute drive east from the centre of Adelaide on a freeway that cuts through the Adelaide Hills is Murray Bridge, a quiet country town that spans both banks of the River Murray, the biggest river in Australia. Like many of the smaller country centres, Murray Bridge suffers from high levels of unemployment and housing rentals are cheap.

Gary O'Dwyer had rented a house near Bunting and Vlassakis in Murray Bridge, and Bunting had been raving on to Vlassakis for some time about how Gary must be a fag because he looked so much like Troy. He kept repeating that he was a 'dirty' who needed to go to the clinic. Gary O'Dwyer was, in fact, an invalid pensioner due to a brain injury from a car accident.

One clear, starry night in October 1998, Bunting and Wagner turned up at Gary O'Dwyer's house as they often did, and after some chat and a few drinks Wagner crept up behind O'Dwyer and grabbed him around the neck. Bunting handcuffed him and dragged him into the kitchen. The same ritual they had previously observed was followed. If O'Dwyer said something wrong, he was bashed on the head. The same music track from *Throwing Copper* was played. O'Dwyer was gagged and the Variac machine, the cigarette lighter and the sparklers were used. Police found among Bunting's belongings a tape recording of the conversation between Bunting and O'Dwyer during the rituals of torture.

> *Bunting*: What are you?
> *O'Dwyer*: I'm a paedophile.
> *Bunting*: Are you glad you've had treatment?
> *O'Dwyer*: I feel really happy that I had the treatment.
> *Bunting*: Did you like the clinic?
> *O'Dwyer*: Hmm.
> *Bunting*: Did you like the treatment you got?
> *O'Dwyer*: No.
> *Bunting*: Did it hurt lots?
> *O'Dwyer*: Yes. It hurts lots.
> *Bunting*: Are you ever going to fuck another little girl or boy?
> *O'Dwyer*: No. I'm not.
> *Bunting*: Now, how do we know you're not going to ever hurt another little kid? You know you'll get hurt, don't you?
> *O'Dwyer*: Yeah, I know I'll get hurt if I hurt someone else.
> *Bunting*: Say hello to the Chief Inspector.
> *O'Dwyer*: Hello, Chief Inspector.

Bunting: Now say, 'I'm a dirty and I'm sorry you weren't here to meet me.'
O'Dwyer: I'm a dirty and I'm sorry you weren't here to meet me.
Bunting: He's a good little faggot. Good little boy.
Wagner: He's trying to be good.

The voice of Gary O'Dwyer on the tape is that of a young man, slow of speech and clearly terror-stricken. Bunting's voice is strong and in control and Wagner's voice merely repeats, parrot-like, whatever Bunting says.

When Gary O'Dwyer's body was eventually removed from the barrel that contained the legs and other body parts of Troy Youde, there were electrical burns all over his body and damage to his scrotum. Splits to the skull had been caused by a blunt object.

The last time Elizabeth Haydon was seen alive was on 21 November 1998. She was living at Blackham Crescent, Smithfield Plains with her husband at that time, Mark Haydon, and her children from other partners. That weekend her children were away and Bunting and Wagner were spending a lot of time there. Mark Haydon was ordered to take her sister, Jodie Elliott, with whom Bunting was having an affair, out of the house on the pretext of buying her a present. When they returned, Bunting said that Elizabeth had made a pass at him and he had rejected her. Bunting told Vlassakis that he and Wagner had strangled her in the bath.

Jodie Elliott now had a son and a sister who were missing, yet she believed every word that Bunting told her. Even though Bunting disappeared for days and weeks on end, she believed him when he said he had a job driving trucks. She was so besotted with him that she did anything he asked of her, even impersonating her sister in order to access her welfare payments. By January 1999 she was in a psychiatric ward, cradling a porcelain doll she had named Jodie Bunting.

Taped telephone calls from Bunting to Wagner before their arrest reveal Bunting calling her 'the village idiot' and voicing his concern that she would talk to the police.

~

It was Mother's Day, 9 May 1999, when Bunting, Wagner and Vlassakis murdered their final victim. David Johnson was the stepbrother of James Vlassakis and was at the time living in Salisbury with his father, Marcus Johnson, former husband to Elizabeth Harvey, the mother of Vlassakis.

Bunting had been on about killing David Johnson for some time. He kept ranting about his being a faggot and needing to die. His plan was for Vlassakis to lure him to the bank at Snowtown on the pretext of selling him a cheap computer. After a couple of unsuccessful attempts, it was finally organised for the early evening of Mother's Day.

Vlassakis asked Johnson to follow him to his mother's place so he could drop off her car. Police phone taps recorded that at 6.40 that night, Vlassakis received a call from Wagner.

'Where are you?'

'I'm just at my mum's house now, taking the car home. Then we're leaving.'

'So you've got pus-head with you?'

'Yeah, he's just behind me.'

'Where's your car? Out of sight?'

'I parked it down near Angie's.'

Friends of Bunting and Wagner had rented the empty bank in Snowtown to them, having been told they needed it to store barrels full of kangaroo meat they were processing for pet food. Bunting and Wagner had previously showered at the friends' house after cutting up victims destined for the barrels.

'So we won't see it?' Wagner said.

'No dramas,' Vlassakis replied.

Wagner, reassured that Johnson was on his own, asked Vlassakis to ring him back when he was leaving. Vlassakis said that he had tried to ring him earlier but couldn't make contact. Wagner explained that was because he was inside the bank.

At 6.56 pm, Bunting called Vlassakis, who answered him with, 'This is the voice of happiness, we're on our way up there.'

Bunting replied, 'Cool.'

To maintain the pretext of the computer for sale while David Johnson was sitting next to him in the car, he asked, 'So, it's still all right for two hundred?'

Bunting told him they would leave the side door open so they could walk straight in. Again for the innocent Johnson's benefit, Vlassakis said, 'The machine's all set up, isn't it?'

Bunting replied, 'Yeah.'

James Vlassakis led the way through the side door of the bank, which was open as planned, and walked towards the computer. When he turned around, Robert Wagner had Johnson by the throat and Bunting was attaching handcuffs to his wrists. Johnson was marched into what had been the bank manager's office and ordered to hand over his wallet and his ATM card.

Bunting, after sorting through his wallet, demanded to know his PIN number. When Johnson told him, he wrote it in his notebook, which also contained the names of Johnson's friends and family. Vlassakis was shown this list and was asked to add to it, which he did. Wagner carried the computer from the bank into the office.

Bunting recited names and phrases, and Johnson then repeated them into the computer, which Vlassakis was operating.

A black plastic sheet was then placed on the floor and Johnson made to sit on it. The ritual that they had developed during other murders was followed. The CD called *Throwing Copper* was played while Johnson's T-shirt was cut off, his jeans removed and he was left sitting on the black plastic sheet in his underpants.

Bunting removed Johnson's socks and held one up to his nose. Even though Bunting had no sense of smell, he sneered: 'Phew, how long have you been wearing this? It stinks. You're disgusting.' He jammed it into Johnson's mouth as a gag and wrapped adhesive tape around his head to keep the gag in place. With the music screaming in their ears, their ritual of violence began.

Each of them took turns to punch and kick Johnson. Again and again they struck him, particularly in the genitals while one of them held his legs open. Johnson screamed with pain but kicked back at them. The more he kicked, the harder they struck him. Red in the face and spitting, Bunting screamed at him, over and over again, that he was a faggot who deserved to die. When they had satisfied their initial frenzy and Johnson was a crumpled, bloody heap on the black plastic, Bunting ordered Wagner and Vlassakis to go to the nearest ATM at Port Wakefield with Johnson's card and PIN number and clear out his account.

Vlassakis and Wagner took David Johnson's car to drive to Port Wakefield but a recorded phone call from Vlassakis at 10.40 pm told Bunting that the card had been cancelled due to lack of funds.

When they returned to the bank they found Johnson still lying on the black plastic, the handcuffs in place. He was dead. Bunting said Johnson had put up a fight and grabbed Bunting's knife, so he had grabbed some cord and strangled him. He complained that his ribs were hurting where Johnson had kicked him. He ordered them to carry his body into the vault. Wagner and Vlassakis put on what they called 'the playsuit', disposable overalls and gloves. Vlassakis was told by Wagner that this would be 'a slice and dice'.

Once inside the vault they removed the handcuffs, the tape was cut with a knife and the sock removed from his mouth. A barrel was selected. After removing his watch, they pushed Johnson head-first into the barrel. Wagner first attempted to hack off the right lower leg at the knee. Bunting kept popping his head around the door to see what they were doing.

When Bunting had gone, Wagner grabbed Johnson's right leg and sliced off from the thigh a chunk of skin and muscle which he placed in a glove.

Suddenly one of the friends who'd rented them the bank appeared at the side door. He had spoken to Bunting earlier and, curious to know what they were doing at the bank, had decided to see for himself. Finding the side door locked he had undone it, only to discover a safety chain barring his entrance. He called out. Bunting let him in. Wagner had already rung the friend's wife to see if they could shower there afterwards. The friend glimpsed Wagner and Vlassakis in the vault wearing gloves and overalls. Bunting assured him they would all be around at his place soon for a shower and he left.

~

Bunting and Vlassakis drove Johnson's Nissan EXA and Wagner drove his own car to Mark Haydon's house, where Haydon and his sister-in-law, Jodie Elliot – who continued to believe she was engaged to Bunting – were still up. Bunting offered David Johnson's car to Jodie for $1500. He said to consider it a Mother's Day present.

~

What of the Crown's chief witness, James Vlassakis? Why did he go along with Bunting and Wagner? Why, at least, didn't he warn his stepbrother? This was the explanation he gave to the court:

I was thinking, how can I stop John from doing this? How do I stop the murder? What would happen if I did stop the murder? If I told John the car had blown up. If I told David what was going to actually happen. I personally didn't trust the police, and I thought that if I did tell the police John would be arrested, he'd be given bail and he'd get me. Or we'd both be arrested and put in together in the same cell. I knew that if I told anyone, he was going to get me. Or if he was arrested he'd break out. I had no faith in anyone and I didn't know any way of getting out of it. I had a feeling it was either going to be him or me at that stage, because of everything that I knew and I was just starting to go into overdrive. I just had to make a decision and that was the decision I made. It was the wrong one to make but I believed that the more John was convinced that I was keen to be part of the plan, the safer I was.

Professor Mullins, the psychiatrist, was able to give further evidence that explained why and how Vlassakis was so vulnerable to Bunting's influence. I'll quote directly from the transcript of what he said in court in order not to misinterpret his professional analysis.

The disorganised and disrupted life which Mr Vlassakis experienced throughout his childhood and early adolescence is clearly a result, in large part, of his mother's disturbances. This is not a young man who ever experienced the kind of consistent care and consistent model from a parent which might have given some strength and stability to his character. Not only did he lose his father at a young age, but he never had a mother who was capable of providing him with a controlled, caring environment.

The other thing about his mother's disorder was that it led

her to have a totally peripatetic existence, moving constantly, which disrupted any possibility of this boy developing relationships with peers, coping at school in any ongoing way, so he was exposed to an inconsistent, constantly changing and ineffectively caring environment throughout his childhood, leaving him vulnerable, dependent and really with very little strength of character. When Mr Bunting came on the scene, James Vlassakis was peculiarly vulnerable to the blandishments of this man. Vulnerable because of his past and recent severe sexual abuse. Vulnerable because of the absence of any consistent caring figure of either gender, but particularly a male, in his life. Vulnerable because this was a boy at that time who had never had the opportunity of a close and ongoing relationship with anyone, other than the rather disordered one with his mother. Commonsense tells us that boys growing up desire some kind of male model, some kind of closeness with adult males, someone on who they can model their behaviour.

It's important always to look at the impact of child sexual abuse in the context in which it occurs and in the context of the person to whom it occurs. Sexual abuse, in and of itself, is a distressing, disturbing and potentially damaging experience for any child. Sexual abuse which occurs to someone from a disrupted and disorganised background, who is already developmentally vulnerable, is far more damaging.

When you look at Mr Vlassakis it isn't simply that this is someone who was sexually abused on a number of occasions. It is someone who was already suffering a large number of disadvantages, developmentally, who was vulnerable because of his childhood and therefore you would expect abuse to be all the more damaging and destructive. He has been exposed to the grossest forms of sexual abuse.

The effects of child sexual abuse are not specific, in other words you don't get some specific post-abuse syndrome. What you get is a profound disruption of normal development. Which aspects of development are disrupted depends to some extent on how severe the abuse is, the age at which it occurs, but in broad terms, what you usually see in those who have been abused, with the severity that Mr Vlassakis was abused, is that they fail to develop the capacity for effective and close intimate relationships, that they have considerable problems with instability of mood, particularly high levels of anxiety and tendency to depression. There's a very strong association between severe child sexual abuse and suicidal and self-damaging behaviour, particularly in the adolescent years and early twenties. There's an association with considerable sexual problems, both in males and females.

In terms of their development there's often a profound disruption of normal development of personality so that what happens is that normal development is retarded and perverted by the impact of the abuse. The depression has its roots in the deprived and disorganised childhood and in the sexual abuse. The effect of long-standing depression during adolescence is, again, to retard normal development. The other thing about depressive illness is that during the periods of depression people become very dependent on others and they become very vulnerable. In that situation they are easily caught up and suborned by others, because they are desperately seeking support and comfort. It's part of depression to doubt and to lack self-confidence. Drug use is similarly a pathetic dependence.

One of the things which struck me was the way in which he was gradually drawn into the world of John Bunting, drawn into it at two levels. One, into the peculiar set of beliefs of Mr Bunting, the threat of paedophiles, his mission to save children from paedophiles. So also, at the same time, drawn into the behaviour involving him in what is essentially

insulting behaviour towards men that Bunting said were
paedophiles, progressing to property damage, then to theft,
then to violence and at the same time introducing him first
to guns, then to shooting, then to killing and torturing of
animals. So that there is in this process almost, I think,
a 'grooming' is the best word. This gradual introduction to
increasingly criminal behaviour, at the same time as being
drawn increasingly into the world and the ideas, which at
least for Mr Bunting justified these acts.

The Crown prosecutor asked the professor, 'Did you observe
distress when Vlassakis was being interviewed?'

In the early stages he was composed and polite but when we
came to his involvement in matters he was very distressed.
I think we can be very confident, immaturity is a very
important part of this young man and immaturity is one of
the few things that time improves. He's a very dependent, to
some extent a disorganised personality. That should improve.
He is still, despite his years, really a young man who has not
reached a level of maturity. There's room for change and
room for development . . .

I'm not sure I can answer [the prosecutor's question about
whether Vlassakis could be rehabilitated]. It's more than a
dependent relationship. He was totally suborned by Bunting.
It's not a matter of identifying with or just admiring someone
or even accepting their views, it's a matter of falling, almost
completely, under the control and the influence of someone
else, so that you come to accept their bizarre and twisted views
of the world as the natural and real world in which you live.
People who have been caught up in these kinds of situations
can take weeks or months to even begin to realise that these
views were foreign to them and that these beliefs are not

theirs but things that they've been caught up in and had imposed on them by a more powerful, more dominating personality.

After discussing the effects on Vlassakis of his mother's degree of involvement in aspects of the murders, Mullins then proceeded to give the background to Vlassakis's life. Again I quote directly in order to give an accurate account.

James Vlassakis was born on 24 December 1979. At the time of his participation in the murders of Troy Youde, Frederick Brooks, Gary O'Dwyer and David Johnson, he was eighteen years old, for the first three, and nineteen at the time of the death of David Johnson. He was born in Adelaide. He's always lived in South Australia. His biological father was Spyridon Ross Vlassakis who died of a heart attack at the age of 49 when his son was only seven years old. He remembers him as an intelligent man who spoke a number of languages, also working as a chef and doing some security work. Separation occurred during the marriage prior to the death of the father.

James's mother has been known by a number of names. Elizabeth Harvey died on 6 February 2001. She was 47. She was born in Australia. She worked for a while as a secretary up until about '92 when her mother became ill with cancer and eventually died. Around this time, which was late '93, she suffered severe psychiatric problems. She had a nervous breakdown. She and her family were reliant on social security from about '92, when she was under the care of several psychiatrists. She was admitted to Glenside Hospital and Hillcrest on a number of occasions. She used a number of prescription drugs and gave some of these drugs to her children.

James is the second of four children. He had three brothers, the eldest who was in fact his half-brother, Troy Youde. He pleaded guilty to his murder. Then he had another brother . . . and then [another]. When his mother was very severely depressed she would withdraw from interaction with her children, basically ignore them. From '92 onwards she was a compulsive shopper. It is believed she suffered from bi-polar disorder, manic depression. She would compulsively shop and also spend entire days playing the pokies. That's how she met Elizabeth Haydon, the wife of Mark Haydon, who was one of the deceased.

After her father died Elizabeth Harvey commenced a relationship with Marcus Johnson. They lived in a de facto relationship for about nine years, were married for about a year before they finally separated. He was employed by GMH Holden at Elizabeth throughout the relationship and by all accounts was a hardworking man who had some of his own difficulties with poker machines. But he was a relatively benign influence. There was no suggestion of any abusive behaviour. But James never referred to him as his father, nor did he consider him his father. Johnson continued to have contact with the family from time to time, some of the children would live with him but James didn't.

They lived at Smithfield Plains, near Elizabeth. Then they moved to Salisbury North, Elizabeth North, Elizabeth Park. She separated from Marcus, living only with the boys. And this is where James suffered significant sexual abuse at the hands of a neighbour. In 1994 he came to meet John Bunting because Bunting formed a relationship with his mother and promised to look after him as his father. Bunting was 28 and James was fourteen. His mother was significantly older than Bunting but she formed a relationship with him and they moved around a lot.

James attended eleven different schools. Despite the fact that he was a promising student, he suffered constant disruption. He attended Smithfield Plains School, Salisbury North Primary School, Settler's Farm Primary School, Elizabeth North Primary School, St Mary Magdalene at Golden Grove, East Marden Primary School, Charles Campbell Secondary School, Gawler High School, Elizabeth City High School, which is now Fremont High, Swanreach Area School and then Para West Adult Campus, which he tried to reattend in '96. He effectively dropped out of school during '94.

Mrs Harvey had psychiatric problems. She said she had been in a physically and sexually violent marriage. She disclosed that her eldest son, Troy, was sexually abused by Spyridon Vlassakis, and so were James and a younger son . . .

During '93, when his grandmother was dying, and his mother was having mental difficulties, they were befriended by . . . a paedophile. When his sexual abuse of the boys was disclosed, his mother mentally collapsed. It appears that Mrs Harvey had had a very abusive life herself. She'd been the subject of both physical and sexual abuse from a young age. The disclosure of her three sons' sexual abuse, caused her to revisit her own abuse and she literally fell apart psychiatrically. It was after that that she met Bunting and he became the boys' father. The family was in continuous crisis from late '93 onwards. It was also a crisis of poverty. The family were existing on social security, separated from Marcus Johnson, with the use of poker machines by both Marcus and Mrs Harvey.

The sexual abuse by the [paedophile] included masturbation and oral and anal intercourse. It happened on an almost daily basis for a few months in '93 and early '94. Often Mrs Harvey would be away at her mother's home, staying overnight. The three younger boys were frequently left alone and that's when [the paedophile] befriended James. He exposed him to pornography and promised if he cooperated that he wouldn't touch his two younger brothers . . . He threatened at some stage to kill James's mother if sex acts weren't performed.

After the abuse was disclosed James learnt that his younger brothers . . . were also abused and he felt, understandably but quite wrongly, that he was in part responsible for the abuse of his younger brothers. He felt great anger for being put in that position where his mother was not there to look after the boys. He found great difficulties in disclosing this abuse and when he spoke to the police he couldn't disclose the most serious acts of anal penetration. He did tell the social worker who worked with him at the Children's Hospital. But John Bunting was the only person he felt he could tell the whole story to . . .

The effects of the abuse . . . were devastating. He couldn't attend school. He couldn't handle what had happened. Eventually he moved out of home because he couldn't deal with the dynamics of his family and the trauma of his younger brothers because he felt some responsibility.

[The paedophile] was eventually convicted of a number of offences. However, when he was first arrested he was granted bail and returned to live in the street. He used to sit out the front of the house and make comments referring to the three boys as his boys. This is whilst he was on bail and there's even a suggestion photographs were taken of the boys by [him].

James said that from that point he had no faith that the police would be able to protect him because when he and his brothers had reported extensive abuse to the police, rightly or wrongly in the eyes of a fourteen-year-old, he blamed the police for this man being back on bail and living in

their street. It was in the context of this abuse that he
met John Bunting, who encouraged him to proceed with
the prosecution . . . and to pursue criminal injuries
compensation for himself and the rest of the family. Bunting
became James's hero.

It is almost incomprehensible to me and indeed, I suspect, to
most readers of this book that young Australians like James
Vlassakis are forced to lead such disturbed, disrupted and horrific lives and to endure such a high level of deprivation and
abuse. All through no fault of their own. Surely not in the Lucky
Country, we cry. These lives, nevertheless, continue to be lived,
mostly in areas of poverty and disadvantage, hidden from the
eyes of the media and the general public. And even when we are
forced to see it, our first impulse is to turn away. Or block it out.

Not that the problem of child abuse is specific to South
Australia. Failure to deal with it in Queensland brought down a
governor-general and a national report showed that child abuse
costs Australia almost $5 billion a year. The costings were based
on estimates of 38,700 abused and neglected children. This
estimate is generally considered to be conservative, given state
governments receive about 10,000 notifications of abuse every
year.

~

The brochure of the Adelaide Festival of Ideas in 2003 stated
that its themes were hope and fear. It did not include specific
discussions on poverty or sexual abuse or the effects of deinstitutionalisation on the mentally ill. The disenfranchised were not
even on the margins of these discussions, although the subjects
of these issues, this book and Adelaide's revived reputation as
a murder capital all lived a mere twenty minutes away by car
from the cultural boulevard of North Terrace.

I'm not, however, being holier-than-thou. In truth, I am not sure that, had I continued to live here, I ever would have asked the questions I am now asking. Perhaps I, too, would have closed ranks, pulled down the blinds of denial or simply refused to speak about it. In a Festival of Ideas, when you have distinguished visiting thinkers from all over the world, as a committee you tend to concentrate on global rather than local issues. I did notice, however, that on the festival program there was a discussion titled Envisioning Real Utopias, a topic close to Adelaide's heartland.

~

The Premier's Office looked as if it, too, had been designed by a committee. The grey, pink and blue flecked carpet was matched by the padded chairs lined up like train carriage seats around a coffee table covered with pamphlets. The ceilings were low, the lights fluorescent and a pretty young girl who picked up the phone every few minutes and chirruped, 'Kimberley speaking' was seated at a centre desk that was curved at its front like a ship's bow. One long Aboriginal painting sat alongside a streetscape.

As if he knew what I was thinking as I waited to be called into his office, the premier's first words to me were, 'I didn't decorate it. My predecessor did and it cost so much that I couldn't justify spending money changing it all again.'

'Fair enough,' I said as we sat down opposite each other, his press secretary on his left.

Mike Rann is still boyish-looking even though he has been engaged in the business of South Australian politics since he first arrived in Adelaide from Auckland in New Zealand during his university holidays in 1973.

Don Dunstan's vision inspired Mike to work and settle in Adelaide after he graduated with a degree in American and Australian politics.

'The Dunstan experiment beckoned to me. Don was the maestro of what was actually possible if you set out to create the exemplar of social democracy. Adelaide was a city-state, small enough to actually see the results of what you are trying to achieve. I saw it as a model for others to follow. Dunstan was determined to create the best possible place to live and give his citizens the highest possible quality of life.'

Mike's first job was in the government's Industrial Democracy unit, which he couldn't believe existed outside of Germany, let alone in this small city in the southern hemisphere. He went on to finally become Dunstan's press secretary. After Dunstan's resignation due to ill health in 1979, Mike continued to work for the Labor Party, finally becoming the Premier of South Australia with the support of Independents at the end of 2002.

Dunstan is still held high as his role model and it is Dunstan's vision that he uses as a template for the city. Not surprisingly, he is determined to revive Adelaide's reputation as a creative city with thinking and talking and collaboration as its hallmarks.

'I am determined to spread the Festival of Ideas throughout the rest of the year. I have provided money for visiting thinkers to come and live amongst us. We have had Herbert Girardet, who is an expert on the greening of cities, to help us plan to plant a million trees. Charles Landry from London is here at the moment working on how we can make a creative and sustainable city, and then Baroness Greenfield is coming to do some work on the brain and Alzheimer's disease. We have already converted the museum to wind power, next week we'll do the art gallery and then Parliament House. It's the creative collaboration that I find so exciting.'

All very worthy and, as the anthropologist Margaret Mead would have said, 'all very pretty', but I was there to talk about the reputation of Adelaide as a city of bizarre murders.

'That stuff about us being the murder capital of the world is bullshit. Statistically, the number and nature of our murders is nothing compared to New York or Detroit or LA. You have to see it in perspective.'

'So why did it get that reputation?'

'It's the downside of being a small city and having only one daily newspaper.'

I reminded him that the murderers and the murdered come from his electorate of Salisbury.

'We are already addressing the kinds of problems that caused that dysfunction. Salisbury used to be a predominantly British migrant town but now it's very multicultural. My constituents are now Italian, Greek, Vietnamese and Aboriginal.'

'What about the widespread unemployment?'

'We are in the process of developing a large defence industry there and already have British Aerospace and Saab as employers.'

'It still all looked pretty depressed when I was there last week.'

'Salisbury North was full of dilapidated Housing Trust stock but we have undertaken a huge urban renewal project and next time you visit you'll see a difference. But you can't turn it around overnight.'

'What about Elizabeth, a failed social experiment?'

'Again, it's important to talk about the fact that we've just announced the biggest job boost in twenty years in collaboration with GMH. It's inaccurate to talk only about its past and how it was. You have to concentrate on what we are trying to do for its future. I have just spent $95 million upgrading the local hospital.'

I had read an article in the morning paper announcing a huge facelift for the Elizabeth shopping centre but wondered if it was just hype. What, I wondered, were they going to do about the problems of the underclass that had settled there?

'We are attempting to deal with the problems of homelessness and mental illness in these areas,' said the premier.

At this point his press secretary informed him that it was time for his next appointment. Having done the interview 'on the record', I told him I would also like to talk to him off the record. He promised me another conversation, before being whisked away into the next office.

Even though I expected him to put a positive spin on everything – that is, after all, the job of state premiers – I could sense in him the same genuine desire to create the best possible society that had existed from the earliest days of Adelaide's settlement.

Is there a virus called Utopia, I wondered?

In this paradise of dissent, what did Christopher Pearson think of the Festival of Ideas? He was bound to have an opposing opinion. I gave him a call on his mobile. He was at lunch, not surprisingly, but it didn't stop him giving opinions.

'There were very few ideas to speak of on offer in this so-called Festival of Ideas. And the ones that were on offer were mostly the scientific kind that didn't particularly interest me. The speakers were just another group consisting of all the usual suspects. The organiser's notion of what constitutes a normative culture is so far to the left that there were no alternative viewpoints. The sad thing is that if there were a real festival of ideas and if there were more of a conscious attempt at the integration of the intersection of art and science, it would be different. And exciting.'

So why didn't he do something about it?

'Quite simply, I can't be bothered. I've got better things to do with my time than be an arts bureaucrat. But if you're going to have a festival of ideas in winter you would think that you would take the preliminary step of making sure that the halls were heated so that people didn't actually have to suffer the freezing horrors of their undergraduate days.'

'If you have so little to do with those who organise the intellectual life of the city, why do you choose to go on living here?'

'I've got my mother and my father to consider, and I have a certain niche after nineteen years of the *Adelaide Review*. If you're published nationally and you've got a network of friends, it doesn't matter where you live. I don't see it as an either/or option.

'If you've got a secure and comfortable home base, it's going to be easier and cheaper to make forays. I've got friends and places to stay in most of the cities of the world that I would want to visit. And research interests.'

'Is it an easy city for gay people to lead open lives?'

'I'm in two minds on that question. You'd be familiar with the argument that it's a city which, even more than the general Australian city, sends its most talented children overseas. Randolph Stowe fled and ended up in rural Kent. One thinks of Jeffrey Smart, who must be among anyone's top dozen international painters in his genre of painting, self-exiled, first of all from Adelaide and then from Australia.

'I enjoyed the benefits of the sexual revolution as well as its disadvantages. And having grown up as an estranged, alienated little boy, I never really expected suburban sorts of pleasures and never particularly keenly felt their loss. I now have the good fortune to be a godfather. One assumes a kind of emblematic presence in people's lives.

'I consider the *Adelaide Review* more of a contribution to the mindscape by extending the realm of the possible for readers and writers than something I did for Adelaide, strictly speaking. Its success had more to do with the city-state demographics and the economics of that rather than the cultural nature of the city itself.

'Those who established this place had a conscious sense of purpose and design in planning. Their attitude was even if it costs top dollar, buy the best, have the best, nothing but the best for our children. And given that we've fallen on our feet in this very comfortable province of the Empire, far away from war and horror and squalor and poverty and class division and all the rest of it, let's rejoice in our good fortune.'

'So, what about the Snowtown murders. How do they fit into the Adelaide story as you see it?'

'To tell the truth I haven't been fascinated by the story. That's partly because of how it has been reported. It's almost as though there've been a number of editorial judgments made about its being somehow not representative, not interesting, and distasteful. One of the things about the suburban character of the city-state is that it is possible, if you so desire, to retreat into an enclave in which that kind of thing simply doesn't interest you. We think, what has it got to do with us or our world? There's a cultural and a geographical divide between Elizabeth and Adelaide. Always has been. It's a story about parvenus and whingeing poms and blow-ins. I suppose that for an awful lot of people who live in the eastern suburbs, what people living on social security do to one another in a kind of Hammer horror way doesn't tell you anything about your own life. It is, in a reasonably plausible sense, not indicative so much of Adelaide as it is of the horror that lurks within the human heart. Didn't Seneca have something to say on that subject? And Aeschylus? We know about Oedipus Rex, so why should we be surprised if it effloresces into that kind of behaviour in the proletariat here? End of story.

'As for going to the Festival of Ideas, I am comfortable enough about Adelaide not to feel obliged to go to any of its public festivals or fetes, in the broadest sense. Partly because I find them claustrophobic with all those people whose names one would rather forget or all those people who unerringly remember one's own name.

A long pause. And then a sigh.

'For me there's always my country house in Delamere, one of the most beautiful Georgian houses in the state and a perfect place to spend summer. I'm also very partial to roast goose in the winter, it's like duck, only more delicate. They grow them locally and they are delicious with mushrooms from the fields. The Japanese war bride who lives nearby still fillets the fresh fish her husband catches, which is standard summer fare.

'Sorry, possum, my main course has arrived. Must go. Ring me later.'

~

After 142 days and more than 120 Crown witnesses, on 11 July it took the defence less than two hours to present its case. Three witnesses were called by Bunting's legal team: one to say that he thought he may have killed Ray Davies after punching him out for kissing him; one, a former drug user and friend of Vlassakis, told the court that Vlassakis had said he was going to kill a teenager and assume his identity to avoid jail; and another former friend testified that Vlassakis hated homosexuals and wanted to kill Michael Gardiner.

Only one witness gave evidence for Robert Wagner. Troy Trengove told the Supreme Court jury that he was the author of a poem in which Wagner allegedly claims to be a serial killer. The poem had been intercepted by prison authorities sixteen months after Wagner was jailed. Wagner purportedly copied the poem and sent it to one of the state's most violent criminals. It reads as follows:

> I'm a CFS [Country Fire Service] man – my uniforms swank
> And I've never been to a Snowtown bank
> Yet bodies in barrels – hey I wonder whos there
> Paedophiles [sic] I'm told so who really cares
>
> See so many people are murdered each year
> Just how many answers can you find around here

Plus everyone's listening to the media hype
A psychotic killer – hey do I look the type

Now in months to come it's my judgement day
You can be sure I shall have my say
And I will not ever be held in contempt
For every one [sic] knows my time was well spent

See you know I only provided a service that's needed
For just like your gardens, our street should be weeded
So fuck off Judge Chester in your silly white wig
I only make the streets safe for all of our kids

Now can anyone say what's really what
For I could be innocent – then again maybe not
So fuck all the media and fuck the police
For I know where you live just incase [sic] I'm released

Now my poem must end with thoughts of my life
Where did this start – what caused all my strife
And if my life reads like a Stephen King thriller
You know I'm not a bad guy –
For a serial killer

Evidence for the defence began at 10.22 am and finished at 12.09 pm.

~

Bunting and Wagner were perched side by side, in their usual positions, Bunting closest to the judge, ready to listen to the closing addresses to the jury by the prosecution and the defence. Not that I could tell whether these past months of evidence had caused any kind of frisson in the accused, so bland were their expressions.

Surely, given the conclusiveness of all the evidence and Vlassakis's damning evidence as a Crown witness, they did not expect to walk away from this free men. What did they think to themselves when they were alone at night, in their prison beds? Bunting, whether psychopath or psychotic or both, was clearly unrepentant. In his own eyes he was a man with a mission. A mission to rid the world of as many paedophiles and homosexuals as he could.

As he lay on top of his bed in the dark waiting for sleep, he must have thought about all those do-gooding, moralising, judgmental people who filled that court every day. He must have known what they were thinking. He must have seen it in their faces.

They just didn't get it, did they? Stupid morons. They didn't understand that he was performing a public service, ridding the world of those mother-fuckers who ruin the lives of children. And if along the way he had to kill some fags, some dumb or fucked-up people, what did it matter? They were never going to contribute anything positive to the world. They were just a waste of space, a waste of oxygen. And if he collected their pensions, what did it matter? By not having to earn a living, it freed him to continue his work. The fewer dirties there were in the world, the better off everyone was. Why should they have the right to live off invalid pensions, after what they had done and were doing to innocent kids? And as for all this carry-on about what he did to their bodies. What did it matter? They were dead, weren't they? Slabs of dead meat. After all, he was a professional slaughterman. No-one carried on about all the stupid sheep and cows he had carved up and defleshed over the years. Oh no, they didn't care about the dead animals that ended up on their plates. These dirties were no better than dead animals. Worse. Some of them.

Anyway, he had to fit them into the barrels somehow. If that rat, that Judas, Vlassakis, hadn't betrayed him, the acid would have eaten away all the evidence.

And as for going on and on about the way he had tortured them. What about the torture they had inflicted on their victims? A lifetime of torture. A lifetime of hurt. He ought to know. He was still burnt up with anger at the bastard who had abused him when he was eight. He was still white-hot despite the fact that he had succeeded in ridding the world of a few of the dirties. It wasn't enough. It never would have been enough. His was a lifetime's mission. He was dedicated. He would have gone on for years and years and dispensed with hundreds of them if he had been allowed to continue. Who would miss them? They were rubbish. Debris. Filth. Their own parents didn't even miss them. Deep down some of them were probably even glad he had taken them to the clinic. They didn't have to wear the shame of having bred them. No-one wanted to own the cretins.

The government should have given him a medal, instead of putting him in jail.

They just didn't get it. None of them. Didn't fucking get it.

And those grinning apes, the cops. Sitting there, staring at him like they were bloody heroes for having caught him. He'd fooled them for seven years and he'd have gone on fooling them if he had gotten rid of a few more of the parasites like Vlassakis. And Jodie, he should have shut her up too. Bloody women. Never trust them. What kind of mothers were they, anyhow, letting their kids get sexually molested? Mothers are supposed to protect their children, no matter what. Cunts didn't deserve to live.

He couldn't lie down any longer. He had to pace. Around and around. And around again.

What was Robert doing? he wondered. Was he sleeping? At least Robert understood what he was on about.

∼

Wagner was lying on top of his bed, his eyes wide open. He wished he could talk to John. When he talked to John everything became clear. And clean. Pure, somehow.

John was the only one who understood what it was like. John made him feel like God, like he was free to act, like he was powerful. He didn't want to be reminded of that cowering, frightened, piss-weak boy he had been before he met John. He'd let everyone fuck him over. Even Barry. John was right. Barry was a dirty who had made him hate himself. Well, they'd fixed him, hadn't they? Fixed him forever. He wouldn't be able to do to anyone else what he'd done to him. Don't go there, he told himself. Don't go anywhere before John. Funny how before John his life was in black and white, and when John arrived it suddenly changed to colour. Bright, bold colours. Every day he saw it all as if for the first time.

John had shown him the way. Now he had a woman and a kid. Now he was normal.

Sitting next to John in the courtroom made him feel proud. Listening to all those lawyers talking about what he and John had done. Made his blood pump. Made him hard. Made him feel like a man.

Those people would never have given him the time of day before John. Now they treated him with respect. Now they took him seriously. His name was in the paper. He was on television. Robert Joe Wagner would go down in the history books. They wouldn't forget him now. Wouldn't treat him like a piece of trash.

John had shown him the way out. John had promised him everything would change. Forever. And it had. So lucky to have met John. He'd taught him everything he knew.

Monday 21 July 2003

'LADIES AND GENTLEMEN,' the prosecutor was on her feet, facing the jury, ready to give her closing address.

'Over the last nine months you have heard a vast amount of evidence which the Crown says implicated the accused. You have heard evidence from civilian witnesses, people who knew Mr Bunting and Mr Wagner, evidence from people who had dealings with them, evidence from police officers, from searches of vehicles and cars and properties associated with the victims of the accused, evidence of surveillance, telephone intercepts, listening devices, DNA evidence, handwriting evidence, finger-prints, pathologists, evidence from Centrelink and the hundreds of exhibits tendered before you.'

While she proceeded to summarise the main details of her case my attention was drawn to the detectives who were sitting behind me and had attended the court for the Crown's closing address. It had been a long haul for them, too; sifting through all the evidence, placing every piece in its right place like a giant jigsaw puzzle.

Perhaps the most illuminating discovery for me was the contents of a U-Store-It facility that Bunting had rented. In it, among hundreds of items, they found nail clippings and a collection of pubic hair (supposedly from V), surgical instruments, syringes, bottles of poison and a quotation, source unknown, copied in Bunting's handwriting.

> The routine of confession that had to be gone through. The grovelling on the floor and the screaming for mercy, the crack of broken bones, the smashed teeth and bloody clots of hair . . .

This was exactly what Bunting had been trying to re-enact in his own violent rituals. The power of the language in the quotation had clearly affected him.

So how had the police finally discovered the bodies in the disused bank in Snowtown?

The prosecution told us that it all began with Elizabeth Haydon, the eleventh victim, who was last seen alive on Saturday 21 November 1998 at her home at 4 Blackham Crescent. At home that Saturday were Elizabeth Haydon, Mark Haydon and his friends John Bunting and Robert Wagner, and Elizabeth Haydon's sister, Jodie Elliott, who was, of course, living with the Haydons and in a relationship with John Bunting.

Late that Saturday afternoon, when Mark Haydon and Jodie Elliott left the house together, they left John Bunting, Robert Wagner and Elizabeth Haydon at 4 Blackham Crescent.

Over the next few days John Bunting and Robert Wagner fended off inquiries about Elizabeth's whereabouts from her family and friends, telling them stories to explain her disappearance. On 25 November Elizabeth Haydon's brother, Gary Sinclair, reported Elizabeth Haydon to the police as a missing person. The next day the police made contact with Mark Haydon for the first time. They asked him to provide a statement about the circumstances of his wife's disappearance, which he did. Then the police requested statements from Bunting and Wagner, who were at the Blackham Crescent address at about the time Elizabeth Haydon was said to have disappeared. Each of them denied any knowledge of the whereabouts of Elizabeth Haydon and provided a story accounting for her disappearance. They were cocky in their attitudes to the police, saying they would have to keep a notebook on all their friends' comings and goings.

On 30 November 1998 the police conducted a search of 4 Blackham Crescent.

There are two sheds on the property, in one of which is a pit to which access is gained via some stairs. On the day the police searched they noticed a particularly foul odour emanating from the area of the pit within the shed, which they described as the smell of decomposing meat. The Crown case was that the shed and the pit had been used to store some of the victims' bodies and property associated with the murders.

Mark Haydon spoke to the police on 26 November. After returning home he was joined by Bunting and Wagner. Jodie Elliott was also home and parked in the driveway of the house was a Toyota LandCruiser loaded with property from the ceiling of the house.

Jodie Elliott had been told by Bunting to stay in the family room, which was at the front of the house, to keep an eye out for the police. She was told there was property that had to be moved before the police searched.

A neighbour observed the LandCruiser was loaded up with garbage bags, placed on a trailer and towed from the premises. It never returned. The police began asking questions and looking for the vehicle. It wasn't located until 16 May 1999, when it was parked with other vehicles in the driveway of a house at 25 Railway Terrace, Snowtown.

On that day, the accused were being followed by the police

and were observed going to this house in Snowtown. At that time they were, on occasion, under police surveillance because their names had arisen in relation to an investigation of missing persons. The police claim that they did not have enough funding to provide around-the-clock police and telephone surveillance, which is why some of the obviously incriminating conversations between the men were not picked up.

Unknown to the accused, Acting Police Commissioner Neil McKenzie authorised the formation of a taskforce, named Chart, whose brief was to investigate the connection between three missing people: Barry Lane, Clinton Trezise and Elizabeth Haydon. By the time it was fully assembled, Chart included thirty-three police from Major Crime, Crime Scene Examination (forensic evidence) and Missing Persons Squad. Supporting them were administrators, anthropologists and pathologists.

On 20 May 1999 the police went to 25 Railway Terrace, Snowtown, and spoke to the owner and his wife. After Bunting, Wagner and Haydon had loaded up the LandCruiser at 4 Blackham Crescent, Bunting and Wagner had stored it at the premises of the owner of 25 Railway Terrace and his wife, then a farm near Hoyleton. Bunting told him he needed to store the vehicle, which belonged to a friend, because it smelt and there'd been complaints about it.

Bunting and Wagner arrived driving a blue Ford. Mark Haydon was towing a trailer carrying the LandCruiser. There was a strong stench coming from the LandCruiser and it was removed from the trailer and parked on the property, some distance from the house.

In the back of the LandCruiser there appeared to be barrels covered by a blanket. The couple living at the farm were told that night and on later occasions that the drums in the LandCruiser contained kangaroo carcases. While the Land-Cruiser was stored at the farm John Bunting and Robert

Wagner visited the property and on occasions checked on the vehicle. The wife, in particular, complained to them about the smell, saying something needed to be done. Bunting told her that they were shooting kangaroos to mince up the meat to be sold as pet food. These carcases in the drums were left over and couldn't be dumped because they'd been shot with an unlicensed gun. John Bunting and Robert Wagner would make jokes about the happy 'roos in the barrels.

In January 1999 the couple living at the farm moved to 25 Railway Terrace. At that time Bunting asked whether the LandCruiser could be moved with them and continue to be stored at their home. They eventually agreed. John Bunting and Robert Wagner assisted them in moving house and in particular in transporting the LandCruiser, again on a trailer, to Snowtown where it was parked at 25 Railway Terrace. This is where the vehicle would remain until it was located by the police on 16 May 1999. The disused State Bank at Snowtown was situated at 30 Railway Terrace, on the opposite side of the road from the home of the couple from the farm. It was, however, over 200 metres from their home with an embankment and some dense shrubbery obscuring the view between the two properties.

As Bunting and Wagner wanted to be able to lock the bank's vault door, the husband helped them fashion a piece of wire to be used as a key. Bunting and Wagner moved the contents of the LandCruiser to the bank and stored the barrels in the vault.

After that time, Bunting, Wagner, Mark Haydon and James Vlassakis were observed by police to visit Snowtown and, indeed, the bank. On occasions they were observed to be wearing overalls and gloves. On some occasions when they'd been at the bank, they'd go to the couple's home to have a shower and change their clothes because they would smell. When the police spoke to the husband on 20 May 1999 he directed them to the bank premises.

On entering the bank the police were not able to open the vault because it was locked. The husband assisted the police in fashioning another piece of wire to be used as a key to open the vault door, just as he had done for the accused. They returned to the bank with the piece of wire. The lock was manipulated and the vault door was opened. This revealed that the interior doorway of the vault had been covered by black plastic sheeting, which had been secured to the doorframe by adhesive tape.

There was a slit in the centre of this plastic from top to bottom, again secured with adhesive tape, and entry to the vault could be gained through this slit. As the police removed the tape covering the slit, a pungent smell consistent with that of rotting human remains assailed them.

When the police entered the vault they saw six large plastic barrels with screw-top lids. Amongst other items there were knives, handcuffs and gloves. Nothing was touched.

The police left the vault with the door closed while further assistance was summoned.

The crime scene examiners inspected the bank and the vault for evidence, and the six barrels were labelled. They were opened one at a time and it became obvious that each of the barrels contained human remains. The process of entering the vault and the opening of the barrels was recorded on video. What was found in the vault and in the bank was photographed before the items were collected and removed.

After it became obvious what was in the barrels, they were resealed and transported to the Forensic Science Centre. There, forensic pathologists and crime scene examiners removed the contents of each barrel and post-mortem examinations were conducted. During this process it was established there were eight bodies in the six barrels. Some of the bodies were in pieces.

In the barrels were the bodies of Michael Gardiner, Barry Lane, Gavin Porter, Troy Youde, Fred Brooks, Gary O'Dwyer, Elizabeth Haydon and David Johnson.

On 21 May 1999 police swooped early and John Bunting, Robert Wagner and Mark Haydon were arrested and charged with murder. On 2 June, Taskforce Chart detectives arrested James Vlassakis. Adelaide magistrate David Swain held a bed-side hearing on 3 July in Glenside Psychiatric Hospital, where Vlassakis was placed after his arrest.

It was the turn of the defence to make their closing remarks. I wondered, given all the evidence, what on earth could be said in order to convince the jury the accused were not guilty. The defence counsel had clearly made the decision not to put the accused on the stand. Given what others had testified about their hatred and anger, and total obsession with violent retribution against not only paedophiles but homosexuals or anyone they deemed 'of that persuasion', it was probably understandable.

Mark Griffin turned to the jury and reminded them exactly what 'the presumption of innocence' means in a court of law. He told them it did not mean 'innocent, as in as pure as the driven snow'. It meant that the prosecution had not proved their case on that charge 'beyond reasonable doubt'.

He referred to the well-known trial of O.J. Simpson, who had been accused of murdering his wife and her friend. He said that if you had just been following the case through the media you might have believed that he was guilty. However, the jury, having listened to the evidence, had decided that something about that evidence – and it might not have been the same thing for each of them – did not satisfy them beyond a reasonable doubt. The jury did not proclaim O.J. Simpson to be innocent, they said he was not guilty because they weren't satisfied that the charge had been proved 'beyond a reasonable doubt'. Griffin referred specifically to the evidence relating to Suzanne Allen and said it would be very hard not to be unfairly influenced by the macabre conduct of cutting up a woman's body when she has died of natural causes. It would be tempting to think that this must be a case of murder because who would cut up a body otherwise?

He said that the major challenge in this case for a jury was to try to separate what they might regard as awful conduct and the legal evidence that the prosecution had presented.

He reminded them that the obligation to prove the case 'beyond reasonable doubt' is on the prosecution. Griffin must have read my mind because he emphasised that the biggest challenge was not to ask questions like, 'Why haven't you told us about that, where is your evidence, why haven't we heard from this person, why haven't you put one or both of the accused on the stand?'

These are the things we expect in a social argument or a debate, but he emphasised that this was not a debate. The rules of law do not require that the defence has to prove anything.

IV

THE VERDICT

Monday 1 September 2003

THE FIRST OFFICIAL DAY OF SPRING. As I clambered down the same rickety iron steps from the plane onto the tarmac, a gust of cold wind bearing light rain cuffed me across the cheeks. I should have remembered how unreliable spring was in Adelaide.

Tomorrow the judge would ask the jury to retire and consider their verdict. At least, those were the words I expected him to say, because that's what they always say on television or in the movies.

I settled myself into a room in the Medina Treasury, similar to the one I had occupied before except this time I was on the second floor with a small deck overlooking Victoria Square. As I didn't expect to be here for long – surely the jury, having sat in that courtroom for eleven months listening to all the evidence, wasn't going to take forever to make up its mind – I decided to treat myself to my favourite indulgence. Well, one of them. Room service is very high on my list of luxuries.

I scanned the menu. Oysters natural or baked with lemon thyme, roasted garlic and prosciutto crust. Seared venison with roasted beetroot and pomegranate glaze, slow-cooked rabbit with celeriac and potato rosti, roasted baby onions and bacon.

The usual range of delights that Adelaide was justly famous for, but tonight with the rain sweeping against the windows I decided on roast beef with a baked suet dumpling and herb butter, crisp green beans and a bottle of red wine from the soft hills of the southern vales.

Gird my loins. Sleep soundly. Wake refreshed, that was the plan.

And I was right.

Tuesday 2 September 2003

I ROSE EARLY AND STOOD on the deck, just able to glimpse the head of Queen Victoria through the bare blackened branches. The air was, as the good folks of Adelaide would say, crisp. The wind still had a bite in it. At least the rain had stopped. The streets were empty. Silent, except for the occasional squish of a car passing.

Plunging my hands into the deep pockets of my long black overcoat, my red pashmina wrapped firmly around my neck, I trudged across the sodden green grass of the square towards the sandstone edifice of the Supreme Court.

Once through security and up the marble stairs to the court-room, I looked around at the empty seats outside and wondered, where is everyone? Lurching through the door of the court-room, I was met by the startled faces of the seated media. Even the judge looked up. I bowed towards him and scurried towards the visitors' benches, my eyes desperately searching for a space. How could I be late? Penny Debelle, one of my journalist friends, waved and made the others scrunch up.

'Started early. Don't worry, you haven't missed anything,' she whispered.

I looked towards the jury benches. They weren't in yet. Take a deep breath and calm down.

Apart from the fact that both the accused were now wearing prison blue, nothing about them had changed. Stone figures flanked by the snow-white shirts of the prison guards.

The judge was going through last-minute details of his briefings with the barristers representing the accused.

Finally, he said to the sheriff, 'Ask the jury to come in now.'

There were three less than when they had begun and, from the look of them, the past eleven months had been a harrowing experience.

The six men and six women who filed into their seats created a phalanx on the opposite side of the court to the accused. Apart from the two middle-aged women, who were well groomed and smartly dressed, the jury looked as if they could have been going to the football, especially the men. In fact, as I had noted on first seeing them, there was not a lot of difference between the appearance of some of the male jurors and that of the accused. They had been sitting together for the past eleven months staring across at the two men who had been accused of the worst serial murders in the country's history. I stared at their forlorn faces.

'Ladies and gentlemen of the jury,' intoned the judge, 'I have concluded my directions as to the law and the evidence. At the most fundamental level you need to ask yourself two things. Firstly, has the Crown proved that the deceased were in fact murdered? Secondly, has the Crown proved that each of the accused was sufficiently involved to be guilty of the murders?'

His tone became more personal and familiar when he told them that due to the extraordinary number of exhibits this courtroom would become their jury room instead of the smaller room normally assigned to the jury, in order to give them enough room to move around. He smiled when he asked them not to touch the little white button situated and secreted beneath the bench and opposite his chair. He admitted that inadvertently he had once pushed it, and the sheriffs had burst into the courtroom and pushed him aside in the belief it was an emergency.

At the end of his briefing he said the expected words, 'Ladies and gentlemen of the jury, I now ask you to remove yourselves in order to consider your verdict.'

Outside the courtroom we milled around as if expecting something to happen immediately. A former student from my previous life as a university lecturer called out, 'G'day, Susan, how's everything?'

'Good God, what are you doing here?'

'I'm a television reporter.'

'I hope you get your assignments in on time.'

'Of course. I always did with you.'

'You're dreaming if that's what you remember.'

'Fair go, Susan,' punching me in a friendly fashion on the arm.

~

Midday and the coffee shop in the Market Arcade was full of members of the media who didn't know what to do with themselves. Even though we doubted the verdict would be delivered that day, the reality was that the jury could return at any time and it was wise not to be too far away from the courtroom.

In between numerous cups of coffee we placed bets in a sweep on when the jury would return. I nominated Friday at 2.30 in the afternoon, my reasoning being that it was a respectable period of time to have deliberated. No-one would think they had been too superficial or hasty in their judgments but it would still allow them time to have a good lunch and return their verdicts in enough time for the Crown to give them some well-earned drinks, and they would get to spend the weekend at home. After all, Sunday was

Father's Day and, more importantly for good South Australians, there were two grand final Australian football matches involving the state's only two national league teams being played on Saturday and Sunday in suburban Adelaide. I thought it was a sure bet they wouldn't want to sit in court at the weekend.

Needing to make some notes and quietly gather my thoughts, I left the noisy café and wandered into the Hilton next door for lunch. The place was full and very noisy, and I couldn't quite figure out who all these people were who were drinking in the usually quiet lounge at this time of day. There was the usual gaggle of ladies who had met for morning coffee and were still lingering, either for the ongoing gossip or because they couldn't stand the silence of the suburbs that awaited them. And there were the huddles of discreet couples who tucked themselves away in dark corners in order to avoid the prying eyes of the village. I was well-versed in the habitués of this lounge, having once spent a year of my life pretending that I was dutifully attending the gym upstairs, which I had tired of after a few sessions, preferring instead to eat cucumber sandwiches and drink gin and tonics in the comfort of the lounge.

But the people who surged around me were not the usual kind of people you saw in the smart foyer lounge of the Hilton. The men all had tracksuits stretched over their big beer bellies and were chain-smoking while downing large frothy glasses of the local brew. They were swarthy and loud-spoken, unlike their wives, who sat quietly by their sides, also smoking and drinking.

This was not the business or arts or foodie crowd that gathered here for conferences or festivals, and they didn't look Anglo enough for Adelaide. Listen to me, I thought, I had been back here one day and already I was judging people by my childhood standards of so-called respectability. My mother would have said they looked 'common', and my father would have told her not to be a snob. She would have insisted that it was not snobbery but standards she was upholding.

'You mustn't let your standards slip,' I now realise is a classic Adelaide admonition. In Sydney they would think you were referring to your real estate portfolio.

Only on leaving did I see the big stand in the hotel foyer welcoming the Greyhound owners of Australia to the Hilton for their national competition in Adelaide. It was the Greyhound Festival. Tourism can make snobs of us all.

For the second time that day, I spied fellow journalist Penny Debelle, and called a greeting. Penny made her way over. She was lean and brisk of manner. A no-nonsense intelligence belied her demeanour as a comfortable member of the Adelaide middle class. She had previously confessed to me that the hardest part about living in this city was that it was 'too comfortable. It is very enervating. You have to fight that.'

'Why don't you while away some time by telling me where you were when the call came through about the discovery of the bodies in the barrels?' (Now how could anyone resist such a tempting invitation?)

Being in the same situation of having to stay close to the courts in case of a verdict and already fighting off the tedium of having to wait, she agreed. Albeit reluctantly. Journalists are always reluctant to place themselves in the position where they are the ones quoted.

'When I first heard about the bodies in a bank in Snowtown I laughed and said, "I don't think that's true but I'll check it out." By 5.30 that night I was standing in the dusk at Snowtown asking the detective in charge of major crime whether it was a paedophile ring. He said, "No, it's not but I can't tell you anything else." For the next two days the numbers of the media swelled and the rumours were flying as thick as the dust. On the Sunday they allowed us to enter the bank vault.

'Now, I've had a very comfortable and privileged existence and I've never smelt death but as human beings we must have some instinctive physical revulsion to its smell. Even though they had removed both the bodies and the barrels for forensic analysis, the smell that assailed us was physically stomach-churning. It wasn't anything like the smell of a rotting cow in the field; that's a healthy cycle-of-life kind of smell. This was putrid. It was as if every breath of air was clogged with it. The smell clung to you. I can recall the exact smell even now and others who were there that day say exactly the same. People were gagging, retching – even the cops couldn't stay in there. The only one who could was my photographer, who has no sense of smell. Just like Bunting.'

'So, did Adelaide go into deep denial when the news broke?'

'That's not peculiar to Adelaide. Other cities block out what they don't want to know. Also, there were a huge number of suppression orders, so there was a limit to what we could tell them. Also, as you know, most of Adelaide's population don't live anywhere near the victims. They felt as alienated from it as the rest of us.'

Her mobile rang. We both jumped but it was just another journalist wanting information.

I checked my message service. Just in case.

'You have no messages,' said the prerecorded voice, at the same time as the Town Hall clock struck three. Do not ask for whom the clock tolls.

~

By six o'clock that night, the jury had retired to the motel where the state had sequestered them and would continue to do so until they reached a verdict. The court had closed its doors and the accused were being held in the cells beneath the courts so that when the verdict was decided they could be rushed immediately into the court to hear it.

I, too, retired to my very comfortable small suite, succumbing to room service again on the pretext that it looked like it was going to rain and I couldn't let the other half of that bottle of good South Australian red go to waste, could I?

Wednesday 3 September 2003

A BRIGHT, sunshine-polished day meant breakfast on the deck and a quick trot across the square to the courthouse. We were all sitting around as if waiting for the birth of a baby. We had the same air of expectancy, the same sense of drama, the same desire for it to be over. Finally. As the morning dragged on and I was wired from too much coffee and too little stimulation, I decided to use the lunch break to go to the State Library to unearth the speech written by the Adelaide writer Barbara Hanrahan for Adelaide Writers' Week and published, according to Christopher Pearson, in the *Adelaide Review*'s Festival edition. If all went well I could be back in the court within the hour.

The boulevard of North Terrace houses the most important cultural institutions, side by side, all built in the colonial architectural traditions of the late nineteenth century. The library is next to the museum, which among all its traditional collections houses the best collection of Aboriginal artefacts in the world. Next to that is the art gallery, which specialises not only in the finest collection of colonial art but has one of the three great twentieth-century collections of Australian art and the most comprehensive collection of British art outside of Britain.

In the same architectural style next door, is the University of Adelaide where I spent three years of my life gaining my first degree. I graduated in the Bonython Hall – the structure that folklore states Kym Bonython's ancestors built in order that Pulteney Street not be extended through the grounds of the university. If that's true, it's a very beautiful, if expensive, speed hump. It was also in the Bonython Hall that as a fourteen-year-old I was taken by my school to a matinee performance of *Saint Joan* starring the acclaimed actress Zoe Caldwell. It was my first arts festival and my first serious play. I was transfixed.

The Adelaide Festival of Arts began in 1960, financed by both the government and the wealthy benefactors of the city, in order that the citizens of Adelaide should experience the finest the arts had to offer. If it was too far and too expensive for most people to be able to travel to Britain and Europe to experience the best in music, theatre, art, dance and literature, then the world would come to Adelaide. And so began the first arts festival in Australia and which, in time, every other state would copy. Adelaide had as its model the Edinburgh Festival, staged in a city roughly the same size, which many believe is the secret to both cities' pre-eminence in the arts. Festivals can become lost in bigger cities, whereas Adelaide has many theatres and other venues in which to stage the events, all within walking distance of each other.

I had always loved the state library with its high-domed reading room and its secret alcoves where you could while away the hours reading undisturbed. When I was sixteen I used to catch the tram into the city after school and at weekends, on the pretext of researching and studying for my university entrance exams. My mother put a stop to this practice when she discovered that I was, in fact, meeting a young law student for long talks on the lawns outside the library. How she came by this information not only confirmed to me the smallness of this city in which I lived but the two degrees of separation between its entire population and my mother and my aunts. It seems this young man had told his mother not just the name of the (he thought) eighteen-year-old young woman he had been meeting at the library but also the name of one of her cousins, who was studying medicine. That was enough for the village tom-toms, namely my aunts' telephone network, to start beating and I was sprung as a sixteen-year-old flirt. Strumpet, my mother said.

Now the building that I had thought so romantic was in the process of being expanded by the addition of a huge perspex and glass extension. The vast room that I entered contained no musty books or dark crevices. Instead there were acres of desks with computers, surrounded by mountainous archives of micro-film. I felt totally overwhelmed and helpless. Adelaide manners, however, prevailed and the assistant not only helped me find the Hanrahan article, she photocopied it for me.

Once outside again, the afternoon light beaming down from the enamel-blue sky, even in spring, made me want to remove myself to a shaded room to read the article in peace. The Medina Treasury was, after all, only a five-minute sprint from the court. And Jenny, the media liaison person appointed by the court, had faithfully promised to ring me the moment she had word the jury was returning a verdict.

Drawing the blinds against the light, I remembered the bore-dom I had felt as a child when my mother retired to her bed for an afternoon nap. 'Come and lie down next to me. You can bring your books but don't wriggle.'

I would last about ten minutes before the silence of the sleep-ing suburbs and my mother's heavy breathing closed in on me. Leaping up, I would run headlong out of the shaded room into the light. The glorious, clear, pristine Adelaide light.

Now in the peace of the shaded bedroom with my mobile phone poised, waiting, next to the bed, I luxuriated in the opportunity to revisit Hanrahan territory. I took myself back to the huge white marquee crammed to the brim with the 1988 Adelaide Festival Writers' Week audience, fanning themselves against the stifling summer heat. As chair of this session I remembered that I had so much sweat running down my face I didn't dare touch it for fear of spreading black mascara across my cheeks. I could hardly read from my introductory notes. Sitting next to me, straight-backed and coolly in control, was the author and artist Barbara Hanrahan. She had an aura of such self-possession and perspicacity that I felt as if I was sitting next to Adelaide's Jane Austen. And, in a sense, I was.

This is how she began, green eyes flashing up from her written paper to judge the effect of her words on the audience.

> Everyone has their own feelings about Adelaide, and they tend to be extreme. It's either Garden City of the South (where flourish the arts and sciences, and all things which spell the culture of twentieth century civilisation), or that ideal setting for a horror movie of Salman Rushdie's infamous *Tatler* piece in 1984 (exorcists, omens, shinings, poltergeists, things that go bump in the night). The Paradise version features the stock ingredients of well-watered plain, enchanted Hills, girdle of green, white-sand beaches, wattle-bird says goodnight, sun draws his curtains . . . The clichés and contradictions were there at its beginnings: Edward Gibbon Wakefield dreaming up his new England beyond the seas, free of the taint of convictism, as he languished in Newgate Prison to expiate an abduction and Gretna Green marriage with a schoolgirl heiress.

So immersed had I become in her words and my memories that when my eyes suddenly fell on my little phone I was gripped with panic. Had it rung when I was reading in my swoon?

Had I nodded off without realising? What if I had missed the verdict?

I snatched it from the bedside table and punched in the numbers for my message service.

The anodyne voice intoned, 'There are no new messages.'

My heartbeat slowed. 'Thank God for that.' But I knew I would have to watch myself. One of the legacies of being an only child is the ability to totally disappear from the world into your own imagination and from there into a kind of reverie.

> In Xanadu did Kubla Khan
> A stately pleasure-dome decree:
> Where Alph, the sacred river, ran
> Through caverns measureless to man
> Down to a sunless sea.

I didn't need the opium, Coleridge's addiction, to transport me. I had spent a lifetime drifting off into my own pleasure-dome whenever my surroundings bored me. My addictive dreamings meant I had noticed none of the signs of the so-called weird Adelaide that had so absorbed Hanrahan. I read on.

> Rushdie's Adelaide in 1984 was a city of arson and vanishing children and awful murder. 'Oh, that someone could be so stupid,' said the then Lord Mayor, Mrs Chapman. 'That such a person could have been in the depths of depression when visiting our beautiful city is probably a reason why he should not come back.'

I wondered whether the lord mayor or the city itself had punished Salman Rushdie for his criticisms. Perhaps Adelaide had put a curse on him long before the fatwah.

Hanrahan went on:

The Premier, Mr Bannon [whom she had previously described as an innocent in Harrison school shoes, his little-boy image lynched by a tight collar, masochistically running marathons for pleasure] said that statistics showed Adelaide did not have a higher rate of 'horrible crimes' than any other Australian state. Yet when the baby animals were slaughtered at the Zoo it seemed a particularly Adelaide crime. The city is so clean, so pretty and so much – despite the cranes on the skyline – the big country town it takes pride in being, that it seems, paradoxically, to suit the more kinky varieties of evil. Even in the daytime the streets of classy North Adelaide and Unley Park can be tunnels, enclosed by green leaves. And so quiet, so secretive; all the people shut away behind their high walls. It's sinister.

~

That night I had dinner at one of my cousin's houses in one of these quiet, secretive suburbs. The only time most of us got together now was at a parent's funeral. Now that they were all gone, I looked around the table and had the chilling realisation that the next family funeral would be one of ours.

The whole notion of family and its importance had anchored us, given us a sense of belonging to a tribe. As an only child, my loneliness and sense of isolation had been kept at bay by regular extended-family picnics and parties. Our Sunday afternoons were often spent at Golden Grove, where my grandparents had been married in the little church that stood opposite the cemetery, and now where my grandmother and grandfather and my own mother and father were buried, together with various family members. During our childhood visits to Golden Grove while our mothers were setting out the freshly baked scones and cakes, our grandfather would carve our names on the ancient gum trees under which we sheltered.

Parties were usually held on the big back lawn at my Aunt Sybil's – who, with a few drinks under her belt, would put on her red tights and prove to everyone that she could still stand on her hands. She stopped doing it when, having asked her husband's boss to catch her legs, she inadvertently knocked him out. Whatever the family occasion, we never stopped singing the family song, our aunts and mothers dominating in their warbling falsettos. The last time we all sang it together was at our Aunt Marjorie's funeral, the chapel ringing with, 'Here's to you and here's to me, this time next year, may we be a happy family, this time next year.'

I thought of poor James Vlassakis. Sexually abused by his own father, neglected by his mentally ill mother, further abused by his half-brother.

No family song for him. No hot scones and cream sponges. No being crushed in hard hugs to soft, warm breasts. No kind words to wrap around his quivering soul.

No wonder he clung to the first adult who showed any real interest in his welfare.

Thursday 4 September 2003

DULL MORNING. Light the colour of lead. A brooding Queen Victoria and not a peep from the jury. The early morning television newsreader announced, 'No news yet from the Snowtown murders jury as they continue their deliberations over Australia's worst serial killings. John Bunting accused of twelve counts of murder and Robert Wagner accused of eight counts of murder, having already pleaded guilty to three, remain in the holding cells beneath the Supreme Court awaiting their fate.'

Tell me something I don't know.

Firmly believing my prediction in the sweep to be accurate, I decided not even to visit the courts but to wait for the call in my room. Nevertheless, I still had to shower, dress and apply enough make-up not to appear scruffy, just in case I had to make a hurried appearance in the courtroom.

I had started reading Ian Rankin's *A Question of Blood* not just because I was automatically drawn to crime novels at this time and he was one of the best practitioners of the genre but because he set all his Inspector Rebus books in his home town of Edinburgh, a city he thought, when he appeared at a recent Writers' Week, not unlike Adelaide. It wasn't just the similarity in size and the contradiction between the puritanism of the majority nonconformist religions and the radicalism of its elites; it was the same emphasis on respectability and the excavation of the buried layers of its opposite, hidden from the casual observer, that fascinated him. He never tired of his own city and relished revealing the visceral fears and hatreds lurking just beneath the elegant Georgian architecture. I looked out of the window and saw exactly the same elegant Georgian buildings. It is Rankin's sense of place that casts a perennial shadow over his stories about the recurrence of evil. He takes us just as easily into the seamy and the privileged sides of life in Edinburgh. As one critic said, 'he strips Edinburgh's polite façade down to its gritty skeleton.'

My mobile phone chirruped its tune. I leapt for it, dropping the book on the floor.

'Hello, what's happened?'

'Susan, it's Jenny. Nothing's happened. I just thought you might like to know that today is Bunting's birthday. He's thirty-seven.'

'Well, thanks for that. Happy birthday, Mr Bunting. Has there been any movement from the jury?'

'None. Not even a question.'

'It's got to be tomorrow. They'll all want to see the footy matches.'

'Yeah, well, who knows.'

'You won't forget to ring me?'

'Don't worry. I'll ring you as soon as I hear anything.'

'What are you all doing?'

'Just sitting around, telling stories and reading magazines.'

'Am I missing anything?'

'Nothing. Absolutely nothing.'

I made myself a coffee and turned on the televised coverage of the US Open to see if the rain had stopped at Flushing Meadows. It was still raining. Bad omen.

The commentator said, 'We're all going stir-crazy here, just sitting around, waiting.'

'I know just how you feel, buddy,' I said to the television. When you start to talk to the telly, it's a worry.

Back to the murder book and DI Rebus.

It was seven o'clock when I finished the novel and checked the time. Crime novels have a way of making you forget your own troubles, as whatever is happening to you is never as bad as what is happening to the people in the book. I checked my message service, just in case.

'You have no new messages.'

'So tell me something I don't know.' Now I was shouting at a recorded voice.

Even though I could easily have rung any of my friends or family to share a meal, I was too preoccupied to make pleasant conversation. My focus of interest was too narrow to be sociable. It was as if I had to concentrate solely on getting that jury to deliver that verdict tomorrow so I could return to Sydney and get on with my life.

My head swirling with images of Inspector Rebus and Edinburgh's seedy streets, I threw on my overcoat to ward off the evening chill. Night had shrouded Adelaide and crossing the square was always like being trapped in a wind tunnel. It was only a ten-minute walk to Paul's, my favourite fish café, on Gouger Street.

Once outside the Medina's lobby, I thought perhaps my sight was failing, everything seemed so dark. The streetlights were spilling their usual amber gloom and I felt as if we were awaiting enemy bomber planes. Why isn't the city beautifully lit, especially the huge squares? What was the point of Colonel Light planning wide streets and green squares in a city that is easy to walk around if it is so badly lit that any woman would feel scared in its streets at night? It was all very film noir. Very spooky. Very Barbara Hanrahan. I must speak to the lord mayor. He, of course, doesn't live in the city, even though he wants everyone else to move here.

I feasted on South Australian whiting and big, fat, homemade chips matched with Mitchell's Riesling from the Clare Valley. (No relation, alas.) It was utterly satisfying and worth that scary walk across the square. Now I just had to live long enough to get back safely. I was sure no-one had been murdered in the square but I didn't want to be the first. It was as if I would attract it merely because my mind had been focused on nothing else. I felt that I radiated the scent of murder and just hoped no-one else was tuned in to those particular vibes.

The late news was on as I entered the living room.

'There is still no verdict from the jury, who has been sitting since Tuesday, on the Snowtown murder case, although today was the birthday of John Bunting . . .'

I flicked the channel to the US Open. 'Unfortunately, it's still raining at Flushing Meadows.'

Friday 5 September 2003

I PEEPED THROUGH THE CURTAINS. The post office clock opposite had just chimed seven times. The sky was still the colour of ball bearings. I snapped on the sports channel. Yes! The rain had finally stopped at Flushing Meadows and the tennis was back on.

'It's an omen,' I shouted. I packed my case, dressed, put on my make-up and made some notes, ready for the call and the quick dash to the court and then the plane.

By midday the sun had managed to squeeze its way through the clouds and, with any luck, the afternoon would be clear and sunny and the jury would have a verdict.

I rang Jenny.

'What's happening?'

'Bugger all. We're all just sitting around going mad. Not a whimper from inside the courtroom. I'm so desperate I'm reading *Who* magazine.'

'I'm going to the market for lunch. Ring me if anything happens. Any change at all.'

'Okay.'

The Central Market was its usual buzzing hive. It cheered me to see the shining rows of apples, pears and mandarins, to smell the roasted peanuts and cashews, to hear the clarion calls of the growers inviting you to taste their produce. I went straight to Lucia's for a hit of their fabulous coffee and a plate of their homemade pasta.

'Susan, over here.'

It was my cousin Chris's daughter, Sarah, who was studying drama at the nearby Performing Arts College. She introduced me to her two fellow students and the next hour passed quickly with her telling me about the parts she had played and the drama scripts she had written herself. I tried to concentrate on what she was saying but was more engrossed in the drama of the impending verdict. Fortunately, she understood why I kept pouncing on my mobile like an over-excited cat with a toy mouse.

'I'm worried that it's so noisy in here I won't hear it.'

'I've never seen you so nervy. These murders are really getting to you. Perhaps you should have a massage,' urged Sarah, trying to be helpful.

'Problem with that is if the call came, by the time I got my clothes back on it could be all over. I think I'll just stroll around to the court and see what's happening.'

'Cool,' they said in unison, glad to get rid of Sarah's batty relative.

I banged into Jenny just after I had passed through security.

'I was just about to ring you.'

'I've won the sweep, you little beauty.'

'No. You haven't won. In fact, no-one has. We'll all have to pick new days and new times. They are going to continue to sit over the weekend.'

'I can't believe it.'

'His Honour has just been in to see them and told them that he didn't want to influence them but if they so wished, they could work from 9 am until 2 pm on both Saturday and Sunday.'

'That means they wouldn't have to miss the football. And neither would the barristers or the judge.'

'That's right.'

'It's a cop-out.'

'It's Adelaide. Relaxed and comfortable, remember.'

Having rebooked myself into my suite for who knew how long, I threw caution to the winds. I had a long luxurious bubble bath and the small bottle of champagne that had been lurking in the minibar. It was still only three o'clock in the afternoon and I had drawn the curtains.

~

Saturday broke bright and clear. No wind. No threatening clouds. A perfect day for football.

On Sunday I had morning coffee with Peter Goldsworthy. One of Adelaide's, and indeed Australia's, leading writers and poets, he is the Chair of the Literature Board of the Australia Council, the authority responsible for giving government grants to authors. Even though he constantly told me he was a writer, not a talker, when I asked him why he continued to live in Adelaide now that his children were grown up and he was financially secure enough to live anywhere, his words sparkled like the sunshine outside the shuttered balcony.

'It's Paradise. Adelaide is quite simply heaven on earth. There's nowhere in the world that I've visited that I would rather live than here. It's got everything. We're forty minutes from McLaren Vale, which is like Tuscany with its soft light, its rolling hills, its wines and restaurants. We're twenty minutes from the Adelaide Hills, which I've eulogised in my latest novel, we're fifteen minutes from endless kilometres of the most beautiful beaches in the world, and I haven't even mentioned the Barossa and the glories of the Clare Valley. It's quite simply a paradise on earth. Why would I ever want to leave? The city has Australia's greatest cultural boulevard in North Terrace. There's not another mile in the country that has all those cultural resources side by side.

'As a writer you are better to be in a smaller city. It's still three times larger than Shakespeare's London. Adelaide is really just a multi-layered village. Where we live we can walk to the theatres, the market, the city, the art gallery, the museum, the library. I love the fact that it's a secret paradise. The Dunstan-led golden years showed what was possible in this small Athens of the South. The bank disaster was a blow but we're in the middle of an arts-led recovery, much like what's happened in Glasgow.'

On and on he went, his face glowing with describing the pleasures of his city. I had heard it all before and it was all true but he had no explanation for how Adelaide had spawned Australia's worst serial killings, even though his own novels lift the suburban rocks and stir up the dark things beneath.

I spent the afternoon reading an advance copy he had given me of his soon-to-be-published novel *Three Dog Night*. It was, as he said, the quintessential Adelaide novel, its opening page a hymn of praise to the Adelaide Hills.

> I am driving Lucy – my compulsion, my obsession – up to the Adelaide Hills for the first time. The day has taken its name to heart: a Sunday from the glory box of Sundays, a luminous morning saturated with sunlight and parrots. Happiness rises in my throat, thick as cud; the world outside the car, wholly blue and gold, seems almost too much for my senses, too tight a squeeze.
>
> 'Paradise,' Lucy murmurs, smitten.
>
> Her voice, our common thought. There might be higher mountains on the planet than the Adelaide Hills, but they are no closer to heaven. Each valley is a little deeper and greener than the last, and each ridge, a little higher and bluer, seems another step in some sort of ascension. Even the names of the steps have a heavenly sound; Lucy speaks the words softly as

the freeway exits slide past, big-print, white on green. Littlehampton. Oakbank. Aldgate. Bridgewater . . .

Each valley cups a single small town in its palm: a church spire, sometimes two, an old stone school, a single aisle of craft shops and Devonshire tearooms and petrol pumps.

As if on cue and in one of those spooky synchronicities that I had begun to notice since my American friend Deirdre Bair had talked to me about her biography of Jung, the phone rang. It was my friend from Oakbank asking if I would like her children to pick me up and bring me to her country property, where she would feed us all a roast dinner of lamb and crisp vegetables in front of an open fire.

As their car executed an elegant waltz through the Adelaide Hills towards Oakbank, Peter's words sang in my memory. It was indeed a secret paradise to whose charms even I, a devout worshipper at the shrine of urban New York, had succumbed during what I liked to describe as my bucolic phase. I recited the names of the trees as we flashed by them: silver birch, golden elm, copper beech, golden poplar, weeping willow – all side by side with the native gums and the wattle scrub carpeting the soft slopes. Even the sound of their names now had a magical ring.

Monday 8 September 2003

THE MORNING NEWSPAPER was full of the football results and there was even a photo of the judge, Justice Martin, himself a former league footballer, sitting in the best seats with members of parliament and sporting heroes. With no phone call from Jenny I dragged myself over to the media room to mourn my fate with all the other waiting journalists. At 2.50 pm Jenny poked her head around the door and said, 'Something's up.' Like rabbits scurrying out of hidden burrows, people were actually running towards the courtroom. Jam-packed, like the first day of the trial eleven months earlier, and $15 million later, after a prosecution case lasting 142 days and a defence case lasting 80 minutes, after 17,000 pages of evidence, after 228 suppression orders, we waited.

Justice Brian Martin settled himself. He told the court that he had been contacted by the foreperson of the jury and that she had told him that they had been unable to reach a verdict on the murder of Suzanne Allen. I suppressed a groan. However, he added, he could put that aside if they had reached a verdict on the other counts.

The jury shuffled into their places. The judge turned towards them and said, 'I received your note saying that you cannot reach a unanimous verdict on Suzanne Allen, is that correct?'

The forewoman stood and said, 'Yes, Your Honour.'

'Have you reached a unanimous verdict on the others?'

'Yes, Your Honour.'

The judge asked the two accused to stand. They refused.

The judge ordered them to stand. They continued to sit.

'Why should we?' shouted Bunting. 'I would prefer that you had told the truth about Vlassakis and the deal he made and the fact that he's getting special treatment.'

It was the first time I had heard him speak. His voice was thin and strangely weak, even though he spat out the words. Wagner sat silently by his side. The guards attempted to pull them both to their feet. They resisted. The guards grabbed them under the armpits but the judge waved his hand in dismissal.

And so, the by now familiar roll call of names began. After each of the names, the verdict was 'Guilty'. Bunting was found guilty of eleven counts of murder and Wagner, having already pleaded guilty to three counts of murder, was found guilty of a further seven.

Justice Martin accepted the verdicts of the jury and discharged them from reaching a verdict on the death of Suzanne Allen.

While Bunting and Wagner remained seated, he repeated the verdicts and remanded them in custody until 10 am on Wednesday 29 October, for the determination of the nonparole period. The guards ushered them out.

He turned his attention to the jury and took a deep breath. The kind of breath that a marathon runner takes at the end of a race.

'It's been a long road, hasn't it?'

He thanked them for their work and praised them for being conscientious, patient and attentive.

'Don't underestimate the value of the service you have given to the community. It owes you a great debt of gratitude.' He told them that he agreed entirely with their verdict and that they should now put it all behind them.

'You did your job extremely well. Be satisfied with that.'

Finally, after more words of advice and thanks, he said, 'You may leave now.'

Within an hour, I was at the airport, waiting for the next plane to Sydney.

~

The following night, Adelaide's local Channel Seven *Today Tonight* program showed an interview with Jodie Elliott, sister to the murder victim Elizabeth Haydon, mother of murder victim Fred Brooks and fiancée to convicted murderer John Bunting.

Jodie Elliott said that the last time she had seen her sister was 6.30 on a Saturday night in November 1998, when they had returned from their craft class on making porcelain dolls.

'In May 1999 I had checked myself into hospital when I saw it on the news that Bunting and Wagner had been arrested. Afterwards when testing showed that my sister and my son were amongst the bodies in the barrels my life had ended, as far as I was concerned.' When asked why they had preyed on the unfortunate she replied: 'To them it was a game. My sister knew too much and she had to be silenced. Bunting didn't like paedophiles and homosexuals. He'd been sexually assaulted when he was eight years old but I didn't know the extent of his hatred. I didn't spend a great deal of time with him.'

She went on to talk about her own life. 'I was an unwanted child before birth and unwanted after. I was forced to be a sex partner for my brothers, for my father. One of my former partners put both my hands in boiling fat. When I refused to have an abortion at five and a half months he pushed me down thirty-two stairs, and I ended up in a wheelchair for two and a half years. The Welfare decided while I was in hospital to take my children off me.'

A whistleblowing former social worker whose identity was disguised claimed that the government department had ignored the extent of child abuse in this area for too long and that the Salisbury District officers had recognised the names of some of the victims as past or current clients. She called for a royal commission or a series of investigations into what had been going on in the state.

The item ended with Jodie Elliott saying, 'How could this have happened? They have ripped my heart out of my chest, handed it to me and said, "Watch it beat."'

The presenter appeared on screen and said chirpily, 'On a happier note, coming up, the self-taught real estate millionaire who will teach you how to make your property fortune here in South Australia.'

~

After obtaining a copy of the Jodie Elliott piece I attempted to ring the local government department that would have dealt with cases of child abuse in this area. I was transferred from one government department to another and constantly told that they couldn't speak to me because of 'issues of privacy'. When I explained, calmly, that I wanted to talk about people who were dead and whose lives had been plastered all over the newspapers, I was told to ring the media section of the department. Eventually, someone from that department rang me and promised to get the relevant person to talk to me. When someone eventually rang, she said that she could not tell me anything about those years as she had only been in the department a few months, but promised to get someone who was there during that time to ring me.

I am still waiting.

Channel Nine's national *Sunday* program had managed to interview V, Bunting's former wife. The woman who appeared on the screen in the kitchen of her Housing Trust house was childlike in her manner but forthright in her opinions. At times she rolled her eyes and seemed to pout but she was keen to show the cameras photos from her wedding album of herself and the young John Bunting cutting the cake, both looking happy.

'The John I knew wouldn't have gone round doing what he did. But there were two Johns. He was a nice person but he did used to throw things, once he threw a glass at me, shattered into a thousand pieces, he'd push his motorbikes over if he got into a real huff.

'He didn't like sheep, thought they were real stupid, he didn't like beef, they didn't have any brains, pigs were repulsive, they stunk, he used to brag about how the animals died and the horrible things he used to do to kill them. If you can do that to animals, you can do that to people.'

The camera tracked over the depressing urban landscape that they had all inhabited, focusing on the interior of the house of Robert Skewes, which resembled a refuse or recycling centre with layer upon layer of discarded cans, cartons, broken appliances and squalor. Skewes had been Bunting's next-door neighbour in Salisbury North and had been an orphan from childhood, existing on a disability pension.

He said, 'Bunting seemed smart. Knew about money and finance. We all looked up to him. He was forceful. Told me, "I want to go out and kill all the paedophiles and homosexuals." But he had a mean streak under his placid persona. Used to shout out "mother-fucker" a lot.'

Barry Lane's mother, Sylvia, told how her son Barry had come to see her, very distressed.

'He said, "Mum, I'm scared. I helped to get rid of a body."
And he cried and said, "What can I do?" I told him, "Tell the
police" and he had a cup of coffee and left.'

V said, 'If I had've told the police and John had found out
about it I would have been dead long before the cops could have
done anything. Even the police believe he would have killed me.
I would have ended up in a barrel.'

The reporter asked her, 'Have you gotten over him?'

'No, not yet.'

'Still love him.'

'Yes. Police say he'll die in jail. I should think he probably
will.'

The good citizens of Adelaide were told in their daily newspaper, the *Advertiser*, that the gruesome Snowtown bodies in the
barrels case was not indicative of South Australian society, even
though the verdicts had brought unpleasant generalisations
about the city into the public forum. 'Certainly the serial killings
were as abnormally evil as they were brutal . . . Just as certain,
this state does not have a mortgage on horrendous crimes nor
indeed serial killings. Consider the atrocious shootings at Port
Arthur, the Hoddle Street massacre in Melbourne or the back-
packer murders in New South Wales.'

Although there was one further accused to stand trial, with
the trials of John Justin Bunting and Robert Joe Wagner
finished, it was appropriate the murders slowly fade into
South Australian history. 'It is time to move on,' concluded the
editorial.

No-one asked why or how these horrendous murders and the
sadistic torture of victims had happened. Surely moving on
meant asking new questions and facing the answers, not merely
exercising the old demon of denial by pretending that these terrible things never happened? Even if Adelaide people flirted
with amnesia, the media in other states would keep reminding

them of it. It was time to ask the tough questions. Time to face some unpalatable truths.

~

On Wednesday 29 October, with Justice Brian Martin presiding, the South Australian Supreme Court heard or witnessed twenty-nine victim impact statements detailing the pain and anguish suffered by families of the victims.

'Do not let them out because they will kill again,' said Marcus Johnson, the father of the final victim, David Johnson. He stood across the courtroom from the two men who not only murdered his son but sliced flesh from his corpse for pleasure and play. 'It has been obvious during this trial that they are the same as they were when they were free.' Mr Johnson, who said he suffered from guilt and depression, also felt keenly a sense of betrayal. 'I invited these men into my home and they betrayed me.'

Betrayal was a common theme in the victim impact statements submitted as part of sentencing. The murderers were entwined in each of the victims' lives. Most of them lived in the same area. Mr Johnson had, after all, been married to Christine Harvey, who later called herself Elizabeth and was not only the mother of David Johnson but also the mother of Troy Youde, and of James Vlassakis, whom Bunting recruited to his mission after he began living with his mother. Jodie Elliott, who was psychiatrically ill before she met Bunting and became his girlfriend, was the mother of Fred Brooks and the sister of Elizabeth Haydon, both of whom he murdered.

'They like to kill. They are cold-blooded killers, so please lock them up and throw the key away. I certainly hope they never see the light of day,' pleaded Marcus Johnson.

Vlassakis's younger brother said that he still feared Bunting and Wagner.

'I am scared of John and Robert, even though they are locked up and stuff,' he said. 'But I know people outside who know them. Even though I've moved from the area, I'm still scared.'

Karen Davies, younger sister of Ray Davies, also suffered from a sense of betrayal because her brother had introduced her to Robert Wagner and Barry Lane.

'I had them in my home. I feel hatred for the people who did this to me.'

Allan Porter, father of Gavin Porter, said he doubted if he had the strength to go on living as he was overwhelmed with guilt because he had not been able to protect his son.

John Bunting read a book throughout the entire proceedings. Robert Wagner, however, stood in the dock and addressed the court by reading a prepared statement.

'Paedophiles were doing terrible things to children and inno-cent children were being damaged. The authorities did nothing about it. I was very angry. Somebody had to do something about it. I decided to take action. I took that action.'

Justice Martin refused to set a nonparole period on their mul-tiple life sentences. He said there had been no hint of contrition from either killer for the 'cowardly' murders.

'Your crimes were premeditated and a number of them involved considerable planning and preparation. I'm satisfied that both of you derived pleasure from the physical acts of killing and the violence and torture that preceded some of the killings. I am also satisfied you derived pleasure from the defleshing and dismembering of some of the bodies. It's not an exaggeration to say . . . you were in the business of killing for pleasure.'

He said he was frustrated that the law didn't allow him to mark the men's papers 'never to be released'.

They were allowed to seek the setting of nonparole at any future date.

'However, I make it plain that I cannot envisage any circumstances which would justify the fixing of a nonparole period in the future for either of you.'

Justice Martin agreed to a request from Wendy Abraham, QC that the case of Suzanne Allen be retried at a later date, to be decided.

V

MOVING ON

November 2003

I WAS STANDING ON the balcony of the Embassy, one of the new developments of serviced apartment hotels that had been built in the western end of North Terrace. Directly below me on the other side of the road were the railway lines, behind them the lawn tennis courts of The Drive where I had played while at the University of Adelaide and, above them, North Adelaide, home to many of the wealthy and privileged. Beyond that was the self-contained enclave of suburbs, home to many of the poor and the underprivileged.

The Festival City had, since my last visit, been host to two major international festivals in October. The first was the Barossa Music Festival, held in the luscious Barossa Valley where music is played at local churches, wineries and restaurants and visitors can drift from one event to another enjoying the pleasure of a Mozart string quartet with a glass of local wine, followed by a meal made from local produce.

This is followed by the Tasting Australia Festival, where a host of national and international chefs, foodies and writers enjoy the fruits of the best that Adelaide and South Australia produces and share their views with the public. It is a celebration of the senses in a city dedicated to exactly that cause. *New Yorker* magazine described Adelaide as 'Possibly the last well-planned and contented metropolis on earth.'

Life in Yatala prison, a fifteen-minute ride from the centre of the city, held no sensual pleasures for John Bunting and Robert Wagner. They spent their days in separate narrow cells in the high-security section of the prison. My aim in coming back to Adelaide was to try to visit them. Several phone calls to the manager of Yatala prison, the Department of Correctional Services and the Minister for Corrections all resulted in refusals. My personal letters both to Bunting and Wagner went unanswered.

It had been hard for the citizens of Adelaide to heed the advice of its daily paper and 'move on' from the experience of having Australia's worst serial killers in their midst. A new media storm had threatened the contentment of the city, starting with an interview given by Dr Allan Perry, a lecturer in Criminology at the University of Adelaide. The headlines in the *Australian* read, 'Degeneracy inbred in stifled city'. Headlines like that would have thrilled Barbara Hanrahan and Salman Rushdie but they unleashed a torrent of talkback outrage, letters to the editor and a public rebuttal by the attorney-general.

Standing in front of the Bonython Hall, looking suitably black-haired and satanic, Dr Perry was quoted as saying that while it was not the murder capital, as it was sometimes portrayed, Adelaide had a subculture of degeneracy that had led to atrocities such as the bodies in the barrels murders. He said he was referring to an increasingly significant subculture of people in the South Australian community whose lives are totally amoral and parasitic on society.

I met Dr Perry in one of the many Italian coffee shops that line the East End of Rundle Street and there, over several cups of coffee and against the noise of hissing cappuccino machines, bashing plates, conversational buzz and Neapolitan ballads, he told me how genuinely shocked he was at the hostile reaction to his interview.

I was confused about whether he had meant to describe the whole of Adelaide with words like 'stifled' and 'degenerate' or had been referring to certain demographic areas like Elizabeth and Salisbury.

'I meant those suburbs in the north, and down south too, in the Hackham and Christies Beach areas, where the cultural life of the community has no vibrancy. It is a life that involves a day-to-day struggle for survival which is generally built upon both social dependency and parasitical behaviour. I think they lack an environment in which there is love, action, humanity, in which there's aspiration, in which there's the real joy of life, the feeling that the world offers them limitless opportunities and all they have to do is work and try their hardest and so much can come to them. The children generally are reared, or often, anyway, in dysfunctional families in which the parents themselves often have a lot of personal issues and problems, and this frequently translates itself to the environment which the children are in and they see the wasteland of human life rather than the beautiful pastures and meadows with the butterflies. And it's not their fault.'

So, I asked him, whose fault was it?

'A society that has coalesced into arrangements that rhetorically advance the proposition of social equality but in a factual sense it doesn't exist and no-one who has the power to really change it has the motivation or dedication to do so.'

Spoken like a true academic.

Was he going to blame the government?

'I don't think so, in the sense that I think that government really reflects the values and attitudes and interests of the population. There are not many people who genuinely are prepared to make a substantial sacrifice to create social equality. They're prepared to support the rhetoric of it in order to salve their consciences from time to time, to cosmeticise some of the more objectionable manifestations of it, but when push comes to shove and says, well, be prepared to give up the second BMW or be prepared to maybe not have a holiday home, in order to create a situation of a redistribution of economic opportunity, there are not many who are going to put their hands up and step forward and say, "I'm all for that."'

His accent was still distinctly American, so it wasn't rude of me to ask how long he had lived in Adelaide.

'Thirty years. Enough to get a little bit of a feel for it. I came here in 1973.'

Why had he travelled halfway across the world?

'They misled me. Whitlam was prime minister, Dunstan was premier. I thought I was coming to a new world. At the time I was actually in Oxford in England, finishing off a postgraduate law degree there but before that I had lived in Boston and had grown up in New York. I saw Australia, and Adelaide in particular, as a refuge from urban decay, from the aftermath of the Vietnam War. A place that seemed to resonate with a social and cultural freshness, an awareness that was extraordinarily refreshing and enticing.'

So was he, too, seduced by the prospect of a Utopia?

'I suppose I was. It did seem to be a blip on the radar screen, largely inspired by one man, Dunstan, who brought out the best in those around him. Problem was, as soon as he disappeared it went back to politics as usual.'

He had clearly been disillusioned ever since.

I asked him whether he actually knew anyone who lived in Elizabeth or Salisbury.

'I cannot think of any close friends I've made that come from those areas. I can assure you, not for any personal reason. It's just that in the ordinary course of events our paths don't cross. And the same applies to Aboriginal communities. I have occasional contact with Aboriginal students but in the ordinary course of events I have almost no social contact with Aboriginal people, which I would very much like to have. But in the way in which the ordinary course of life goes here, circles are very tight and unless you make a real concerted effort to break out of it, you are in isolation.'

How had he felt about the attorney-general's anger at his comments?

'Basically, it's no different from any other state. Politicians like to talk tough but rarely think smart because the problems associated with crime are invariably intertwined with a wide range of factors which create dysfunctional subcultures. These things are extraordinarily difficult to properly understand, let alone to have any kind of perceptible impact on.

'They quickly recognise that it's in the way-too-hard basket. Without wanting to seem a cynical person, because I don't think I am, I think most politicians look upon their occupation as really being in a business of winning and keeping power and most of their calculations are based on that bottom line. They rarely think longer than – they say the next election, but I don't think they think longer than six months in advance in most cases. And their main mechanisms for retaining power are rhetoric and money, and they can't possibly see how spending money on genuine efforts at the social rehabilitation of these areas and their infra-structure can possibly be a sound investment.'

'They just resort to beating the law-and-order drum?' I suggested.

'And it's a dangerous drum to beat. One of the things that politicians don't realise is that their self-serving, politically expedient rhetoric may actually have some effect and influence, beyond that of simply winning an election with a lot of emotional rhetoric about law and order. They go in, all guns blazing, and don't recognise the fact that out there, there may be a thousand John Buntings who hear what they say and in their own warped, psychotic minds are happy to take up the mantle of vigilante-ism to help rid society of all those who are seen as being evil. Now, no-one has any sympathy whatsoever with those who abuse others, whether they be children or adults, in any way, shape or form. But this retributive vigilante-ism can so easily get out of control. The stigmata which are used to identify the evil often, of course, bear no rational connection to it.'

Like confusing paedophilia with homosexuality.

'The notion that somehow there's a connection is an absurd proposition. If anything, statistics reflect the fact that it is hetero-sexuals that are involved in a much higher pro-rata involvement in paedophilia than occurs with homosexuals. But those who are alienated, frustrated, who have a tremendous spiritual malaise of pain and agony, they need scapegoats and these are served up to them all the time by those who should know better. And this is one of the great harms that the ill-considered rhetoric of so many politicians produces.'

I asked him how he thought they should talk about such crimes.

'We need to find some way of producing a system of restora-tive justice that can both meet the needs of the victims while trying to bring the offender back into the community. The retributive philosophy of criminal justice that is so glibly espoused by law-and-order politicians only further polarises the offenders and victims, only further ensures that recidivism and re-offending will occur and that long-term bitterness and pain will be suffered by the victim. There's nothing in their rhetoric that brings people together.

'I am convinced that nobody cures the spiritual and psycho-logical pain that is the product of abuse through hate and retribution. Those are not the emotions that bring out the best of people. They've got to find some way to follow a more positive path. A path of compassion, understanding; love, even. And that is hard. Hate is easy, love is hard. Those who know better should encourage it rather than exploiting the lowest common denominator of human nature. My feeling is that the Buntings, the Wagners and so on, are just manifestations of this and they are statistical certainties within this cauldron of forces.'

Like disasters waiting to happen.

'You can't constantly throw acts of retribution or hate into the social recipe without producing a fair number of equal by-products.'

So why did he think we were so addicted to denial?

'As long as people try to treat, whether it's a Bunting or a Wagner or a Hitler, as simply some kind of genetic freak, they are engaging in exactly the self-denial that you talk about. These people are products of a psycho-social cultural environment in which they are bred, and that is what my original interview with the ABC that set this off was intended to raise. A discussion about just those kind of things.'

But surely he knew how carefully he had to tread?

'I might be, and I obviously am, somewhat naïve because I never imagined that it would strike such a sensitive chord.'

I put it to him that he'd produced the opposite effect from what he'd intended. He had closed down minds instead of opening them.

'What I wanted to bring out was that there are many social problems that have been ignored in western society for a long time, particularly in what I would describe as the post-modern era, the era that started after the Vietnam War with the technology, affluence and significant change in social and cultural structures and ideas. For example, the family structure and rearing children that was perfectly satisfactory in an era in which the nuclear family and conformism was so ubiquitous that it was a good workable system for then. Now that's no longer the case and so we have to rethink how we rear children.'

My response was that surely the newspapers are full of those issues every day.

'It's just been finding immediate short-term solutions – "We'll have a day care centre and stick them in it." I think the notion of expanding the educational system and bringing children into communal contact with other children at a much younger age is probably a good thing, but it should be done in some kind of organised, coherent way. We haven't thought about any of those things. We haven't thought about the tremendous problems that technological development has had on the vocational, occupational and socioeconomic system.'

Did he mean comments like 'the rich are getting richer and the poor are getting poorer'?

'I sit here today, I can't tell you a single thing that I can see that's been done to address that kind of problem. Not a single thing. All they ever talk about is the social welfare state ticket that will provide the absolute bare minimum, the bare modicum of support to avoid people falling into a third-world existence. But nothing that genuinely looks at the problem and says, "How can we try to ensure that we have a society that provides an opportunity for everyone to have a purposeful, meaningful, fulfilling life, without being subjected to hate, vilification, ostracism, because of their race, because of their ethnicity, because of their sexual orientation – all things that are so fundamentally relevant to anything that's important?"'

I asked him whether he ever felt his ideas were just what was now labelled a rather unfashionable social idealism.

'It's not a matter of simply saying that the status quo is being maintained. Things will fall apart. If you're not at least keeping up with it, you're falling further behind and the problems are becoming more endemic, more entrenched.

'It seems to me it's like a lawn where you don't properly treat the weeds. This will be easy to take out of context and make me seem like a real lunatic, but, eventually, if you don't treat them, you're left with no recourse but to get out the rotary hoe and dig up the whole thing and start again. I get the feeling here that if things continue the way they are, you'll end up with a society in which basically there'll be a wall built – and I'm not just speaking figuratively here, it's already starting to appear in different ways – where people simply erect both physical and social barriers to preserve their quality of life and tranquillity from the dispossessed. And it doesn't have to be masses, as Al Qaeda and other groups have shown. It only takes a small, dedicated minority in society to create social chaos. If you have a disaffected 20 or 25 per cent of your population, social stability is impossible. And so, at that point I can easily see society throwing its hands up and saying, "Let's just write them off."'

How bad really was the reaction to his statements?

'The situation did reach a peak of what I would describe as lunacy. The police contacted me and offered me protection.'

'Why?' I was stunned.

'They said their police intelligence indicated to them that there was a credible threat to me, and offered me protection. I declined it because I could not believe that this was a genuinely serious possibility. I was astounded at what other people told me they were hearing on talkback radio.'

But didn't he know how sensitive Adelaide is? Didn't he understand what happens when you criticise a Utopia? Didn't he know our history?

'I didn't realise what a sensitive nerve it was, and how much self-delusion exists. And self-delusion is a terrible thing because it prevents you from acting in a rational way. For example, my understanding is that someone tapped the Dean of the Law

School on the shoulder at the university and said, "What do you think we should do about this?" And he told me that he told them: "What do you mean, what should we do about this? This is a university. People should have the freedom to express opinions on things." And they said, "Oh, I guess that's right." And they backed off.

'I couldn't believe it. I've done over the last thirty years, I would say 500 media comments of one sort or another. Most are thirty-second grabs, some are more in-depth interviews. Criminal justice is an issue of perennial interest to the media. And in all that time, all of those interviews, all of those comments, have rarely elicited more than a murmur. I did this interview with the ABC as some background for a special that they were going to put together once the verdict came down. To be honest with you, I won't say I'd forgotten about it, but if you had asked me I would have thought that it had already been broadcast. And so it was more than a little surprising when I came into my office on the Tuesday morning, turned on my computer as I normally do and clicked onto my email, and there were all these little highlighted black emails. Normally, I get half a dozen. Instead there were forty. The voice-mail light on my phone was blinking red and there were either telephone messages or emails from literally every media outlet in Australia. Radio stations from every state. Local TV stations. Magazines. Newspapers. *Sydney Morning Herald*, Melbourne *Age*. For some reason this had hit a resonant chord with them.

'Had I thought that there would be this reaction, I would have been very tempted not to do it because I don't enjoy the kind of public controversy that this produced. It's not in my nature any longer to get into slanging matches with people.

'I believe that this is an important social issue that should be more widely discussed. I do not suggest that my views on this are all necessarily right. I certainly don't suggest that I have the answers. What I am certain of is that it is a social issue of vast importance that should be much more actively debated, rather than the community wasting its time in its repetitively purposeless pursuit of individualised vigilante justice in specific cases and worrying about what happens to this offender or that victim or about this particular incident. That energy should be much more productively channelled into considering the far broader issues.

'If I can see this and recognise it, there are other people out there, brighter than I, who must see it too.'

Finally, I asked him what he now hoped to achieve.

'Eventually I hope people will come to the conclusion that perhaps this retributive vigilante philosophy is not the one that ought to be pursued. That may start bringing about that moment of epiphany when people say: "Maybe the path of hate and violence and anger is not the right path. Maybe there's another way, maybe there's a better way and maybe we should look for some form of reconciliation. Maybe many of those who resort to crime and violence are people who do so because of their sense of helplessness and frustration and spiritual malaise. Maybe we've got to reconcile them back into the community."'

'Surely,' I said, 'it's too late to do this with some people who are psychopathic in their hatred and their damage? People like Bunting and Wagner. The judge certainly thought they were way past rehabilitation.'

'Sometimes it is. But we have to find a way of not producing more of these subcultures – or at least dealing with them. You can't just go on ignoring the problems and pretending they don't exist just because you don't live next door to them. Denial and hostility to criticism is not the answer.'

~

I knew I had just heard an entire lecture on criminal justice, which Dr Perry had probably given often. Nevertheless, it was a lecture that he should definitely give at the next Festival of Ideas. Ironically, especially given the reaction to Dr Perry's interview, so much of what he had to say was perfectly in accord with our earliest beginnings as a 'paradise of dissent'.

We need to have more, not less, of these discussions. Adelaide must lead the way in confronting these social and economic problems, just as it did in the Dunstan decade. In an age of economic rationalism, social idealism needs to be resurrected. Taken out of the dusty drawer marked 'too old-fashioned and sentimental'.

Much less controversial but similar in content was an article in the *Adelaide Review* by local journalist and lawyer Michael Jacobs. He tackled head-on the notion that Adelaide has some special capacity for generating horrors and bizarre murders. He believed such theories only exist because Adelaide is, for its size, remarkably easygoing and pleasant and, as such, vulnerable to myths about dark underbellies.

Denial of such things, he also believed, is equally inevitable. What he wanted to explore was how we could make use of such a reminder of the human potential for evil. In other words, how could this horrendous occurrence be used to stimulate us to think more widely about the underlying issues?

He says, 'It is beyond doubt that entrenched unemployment and deprivation plays a role in adding to the amount of alienation, isolation, indifference to social norms, dysfunctional and disastrous behaviours. This is not a South Australian problem, not even an Australian problem. It is a problem of the present phase of what is sometimes cutely called post-industrial society.'

Aware of the dangers of merely closing ranks and 'moving on' he concludes his piece by saying that, 'if you do not look the beast in its face and call it by its name, you stand a very good chance that, in its own time, it will bite you on the backside.'

~

I walked back to the Embassy; past the groups of people sprawling under the umbrellas outside the endless cafés and restaurants that filled the city; down the cultural boulevard; past the avenging angel of the war memorial, where my little family of three huddled in the darkness every Anzac Day for the dawn service; past Government House, where I had downed many a good gin and tonic; past Parliament House, many of whose occupants I had interviewed over the years. I strode on, past the railway station whose Grand Hall was now the Adelaide Casino, past the Hyatt and the Convention Centre, and finally crossed the road to my gleaming new hotel.

'Any messages?' I asked the young man smiling at me behind the reception desk. Not that I really expected to be granted permission to see Bunting or Wagner. There was still another trial to deal with the murder of Suzanne Allen and yet another for Mark Haydon, who had been remanded in Yatala since his arrest in May 1999. No-one wanted to take any risks regarding suppression orders and pave the way for a retrial.

'No messages,' he replied and sensing my disappointment said, 'Have a drink in the bar. It will cheer you up.'

'What a wise young man you are,' I said.

But I still wanted to meet one or both of the convicted murderers, face to face. I'd had secret conversations with people who shall remain unnamed, who had met them, and had been advised by them not to make myself known. Believe me, I was in no hurry to be Jodie Foster's Clarice to Anthony Hopkins' Hannibal Lecter. On the other hand, when I had asked one of the arresting detectives outside the courtroom what Bunting was really like, he'd replied, 'He's a pathetic little punk. A nothing. No-one for you to be worried about meeting.'

~

It was rissoles and mash again for dinner in the high-security B Division of Yatala prison.

'Not like those Big Macs we'd polish off after taking the dirties to the clinic, eh, John?' They were taking one of their walks outdoors. Wagner found it hard being locked up, alone, for fourteen hours a day.

He was worried about the fact that Bunting had not smiled or even looked him in the eyes for over a week. It just wasn't like him. When the trial had been on he was so upbeat. He'd laugh about the expressions on the faces of the morons in the court-room and joke about what he'd do to some of them if he ever got the chance. He had nicknames for them, like 'pus-head' and 'scab-face'. Used to call that fat cunt Haydon those names all the time. And spit in her hair behind her back. She must have heard him do it. Stupid, ignorant pig of a woman.

Oink, oink, that's what John'd say. Oink. Oink. We laughed a lot, then.

'What are you grinning about?' growled Bunting as they walked around and around the exercise yard. They had already been there nearly an hour and this was the first time Bunting had spoken. Wagner knew better than to interrupt his silence.

'Did you eat your rissoles?'

'Shit.'

'I ate mine.'

'If you want to eat crap, go ahead. I've seen more appetising things inside the bogs I've been cleaning today.'

Wagner snorted.

'Gotta keep up me strength. Can't afford to get soft in here.'

'Wastes. Losers. Dirties.'

'They've had some big names in here, they reckon.'

'Like who?'

'Von Einem.'

'Pervert. Dirty.'

'Miller.'

'Picked on teenage girls. Some killer.'

'Yeah, we're bigger names than them.'

Bunting looked up from the ground he had been fixated on and stared at Wagner. It was a long, metallic stare, as cold and sharp as the knives he had kept from his days at the abattoir.

Wagner felt his cheeks burning and mumbled, 'You're the biggest name, John. Everybody says so.'

Bunting pointed to Wagner's T-shirt. 'Scrape off that mashed potato. Your dog was a cleaner eater than you.'

Wagner looked down, flicking off the stray lump of grey potato. 'You're Australia's top serial killer. The best.'

Bunting said, ignoring him, 'Did you get that information?'

'Not yet, John. But I will. I promise you. I will.'

Wagner smiled down at the stocky little figure beside him. Bunting was busy scraping some of the discarded mash off his shoe.

~

George Gross and Harry Who (Watt) are two of Australia's top fashion designers and couturiers, and who recently celebrated 30 years in the rag trade with a huge gala lunch at the Hyatt in Adelaide, attended by thousands of women who had worn their clothes and relied on their taste for all of that time. They have turned down many opportunities to base their industries in Sydney and internationally. They have rejected all offers to move for one simple reason: they love Adelaide.

Harry was born here, and when he and George decided to live and work together, there was no question that George would move from Sydney. For Harry, Adelaide was and is non-negotiable.

I met them in McLaren Vale on the veranda of D'Arry's, a restaurant inside the D'Arenberg Winery, one of the earliest in the Southern Vales, which in the last twenty years had fulfilled its Mediterranean promise. It's all olive and ochre on this blissful day, the kind of day that you want to bottle and cork and keep with you forever.

The winery was established in 1912 from a classic Adelaide contradiction. The winnings from Joseph Osborn's racehorse, Footbolt, were enough to buy the land for the vineyard, even though Osborn was a teetotaller. Footbolt's name is one of D'Arenberg's prize Shiraz wines. Osborn's grandson, D'Arry, took over the winery in 1957 and his son, Chester, has been responsible for the facelift during the last fifteen years and for continuing the distinctive names of the wines. Money Spider Roussanne, for example, is named after the money spiders that covered the vines of the first vintage of roussanne. Folk wisdom has it that money spiders bring good luck and must not be killed, so Chester left that vintage on the vine and called the first release after them. My favourite red, Laughing Magpie – Shiraz with a dash of Viognier – was so named because Chester's daughters couldn't pronounce 'kookaburra' so they called the bird 'the laughing magpie', which is black and white, like the black and white grapes that make the wine. Dead Arm Shiraz owes its name to a fungus in the oldest vines that can cause some branches to be amputated. The age of the vines is responsible for the concentration of the flavour and high price of the wines.

George and Harry were their usual energetic and charming selves. George, dark-haired, European; Harry, blond and Aussie, both dressed in elegant cool linen.

'Just look at this,' exclaimed Harry, 'have you ever seen anything more perfect? Every time we go to Tuscany we think of this.'

The view from the veranda was of a cloudless blue canopy looking down over lush vineyards and soft rolling hills burnished in the afternoon sun. Beyond them lay the sparkling gulf of St Vincent, the source of the menu's fresh prawns. My attention had already been captured by the vanilla panacotta with grilled peaches but I forced myself to wait. We all started with a tangy linguine marinara in a tomato and chilli sauce.

The restaurant was full of people from Adelaide who had made the forty-minute drive south for a few glasses in the tasting room to choose what to go with their lunch. Extra tables were added to the veranda to accommodate late arrivals without bookings. The service was traditional Adelaide: polite, prompt and professional. No trendy pretensions and no instant intimacy. The galvanised iron roof and hardwood beams of the restaurant blended perfectly into the original homestead cottage of the 1880s. It was tasteful, restrained.

'Now,' said George, 'Why on earth are you writing about these terrible murders?'

'Oh, don't start on that. I don't suppose you two even know much about them.'

'Why would we want to?' said Harry.

'That's such a British habit of averting your eyes from unpleasant things and just pretending all is well.'

'I'm hardly British,' said George, laughing. His formative years were spent in post-war communist Hungary, having been reunited with his Jewish parents, who had survived time spent in Auschwitz, arriving in Sydney after the failed 1956 uprising.

'No, but you've been here so long you have become one of us.'

'Well, I was born here,' said Harry, with more than a touch of pride, 'and the only reason I left was because I thought I was the only gay person here. I'd done my national service in the Navy in Melbourne and I had five years there, but I came back and settled in Adelaide in 1965 and just got to know more and more people, some who were gay, some not. I always found Adelaide a calm city and very pretty. I love the Victorian buildings and the Georgian architecture and the way it is so well laid out. Not long after I came back I had a job as a travel agent and even though I used to fly around a lot I always found that I liked the Mediterranean countries best. And then I came back and looked at Adelaide and realised it's exactly the same. It's very European, look at it. The wine's better here now, though, I think.'

And on cue, we all had a big slurp of the chilled Money Spider.

George gave one of his big beaming smiles and said, 'I loved it from the first time I saw it. Of course, I would be happy with Harry wherever we lived as long as we were together but I could see why he thought his hometown was so special.'

'The first time he came to stay with me, he said something very funny and one of my dearest friends leaned over and said, "He'll do."'

'And we are still all friends,' added George.

Warming to the conversation as much as to the main course, Harry was keen to continue.

'In Sydney people move on from their friends as quickly as they move on from a restaurant. They don't care. They're very superficial. I could never understand it.'

I remembered the day I bumped into them in a North Adelaide supermarket and blurted out that I was moving to Sydney. Even though they understood that if I wanted to extend my media career I needed to move, I noted the hurt look in their eyes.

'It's not forever,' I'd assured them. But I now realise that they like to have their friends nearby.

'Here we have our friends and the kids of our friends as well and we include them in our parties. I don't think it would happen anywhere else but in Adelaide. I guess it was like my parents and me in that we all got on well and we all partied together. I like that sense of continuity.'

The time and the setting weren't right for talking about the murders, and I decided to keep that topic for drinks when we returned to their city apartment.

Needless to say, the vanilla panacotta met all my expectations, and I even managed a taste of Harry's white chocolate semi-freddo with summer berries and almond wafer.

On a clear day you could sit on this veranda forever. As long as you didn't explode first.

~

Back at Harry and George's apartment, I explained to them the background to the book. Harry, with his usual frankness, said, 'I sometimes think I'm fairly intolerant of anyone north of Enfield. They're not the same. Perhaps I'm becoming a snob in my older years.'

'I don't think that's right, Harry,' said George. 'You've never been a snob. It's more a question of never coming into contact with people who live in Elizabeth and around there. It's an enclave all of its own and I guess that's why it's so easy to ignore all their problems. Most people in Adelaide simply have no connection with them.' He added, 'Adelaideans don't travel far within their own city.'

Surely that was true of most cities. People stayed within their own small villages, venturing out on short visits to eat or drink, and visit the beaches or the hills or the wineries.

I sometimes think I see more of people I knew in Adelaide now that we all seemed to have congregated in the same small section of the eastern suburbs of Sydney.

'Who else is in this book?' asked George.

'Well, there's Kym Bonython and Pam Cleland and . . .'

'The last time I saw Kym he was organising his funeral,' piped up Harry from the depths of his cushions. 'He said, "I've worked out the solo." I said, "What is it?" and he said, "Please don't talk about me when I'm gone."'

George laughed and propped himself up on his elbows.

'Do you know you can still park out the front of practically anywhere you want to go?' he observed. 'How many cities are there where that's still possible? Are you interested in going somewhere for dinner later?'

I groaned. 'Are you crazy? You're going to have to get a cherry picker to lift me out over the roof deck as it is.'

Harry said, 'You know we had a friend here the other night and we were strolling back from one of the dozens of restaurants around here and I said, "Isn't it nice to still see some light in the sky?" He scoffed and said, "You mean the football lights." I said, "You will have to apologise to me for that." And he did. Adelaide twilights are just amazing. And down at the beach, the glorious sunsets. Well, you'd know. You lived on the coast for a while.' They opened another bottle of wine and seemed to be getting their second wind.

George, placing a little Greek dip and biscuits almost under my nose, murmured in my ear, 'There is not a minute of the day in which you can't get a drink and something delicious to eat. You could ring a handful of restaurants, and say, "Look, I'm going to the theatre, I can't get there before perhaps a quarter to eleven or eleven o'clock." It's probably going to be open anyway, but they'll hold the kitchen for you.'

'Do you know my favourite phrase when I visit Sydney on business?' asked Harry

'No.'

'Take me to the airport, driver.' They both snorted.

'Speaking of which, could someone call me a taxi? I can't eat or drink another thing. Don't try and tempt me out for dinner, you naughty boys.'

'But the night's still young and it's all only walking distance away, and —'

'On second thoughts, call me an ambulance.'

'Lost your stamina since you've been in Sydney. Time you came home.'

~

It was roast beef congealed in lumpy gravy and soggy vegetables for dinner in B Division. John Bunting and Robert Wagner spent four-teen hours of every day, alone, locked in their two-metre-wide cells. They were not permitted to work near workshops or kitchens or anywhere they might have access to tools or knives. They could earn $5 a day scrubbing communal toilets. If they chose not to work, they earned a $12 per week unemployment benefit, $3 of which was paid into a victim support fund. They were allowed two hours a day outside and a two-hour visitation each fortnight.

Wagner missed Bunting more than he had ever missed anyone in his life. Not that he could ever tell him. He'd think he'd gone queer again. Wouldn't take long in here. Just as well he had John to protect him from his past. They made lick-ing and slurping noises at him when John wasn't around. Sometimes John wouldn't come outside for days. No sign of him today.

'Where's the slaughterman?' they'd hiss and try to grab his balls. They never spoke to John like that. As Australia's top serial killer, he had respect.

There was that rapist John had told him to talk to when he had the chance. He didn't want anyone to see him doing it. They watched everything you did, every eye contact you made.

He was tired today. Practically no sleep last night. Nothing but sweaty nightmares. He put a T-shirt in his mouth before he went to sleep so they wouldn't hear him shouting. Sometimes when he woke up his cheeks were wet with tears. Always the same dream. He was eight and the man was raping him. It hurt and he kept screaming stop, stop, please stop but no-one heard him and the man kept grunting and thrusting and he couldn't move.

Then he had the razor blade and he was cutting his wrists in the bath and watching the white skin part and the water turn pink and then bright red and then the red face of the man loomed over him and it all started again. He screamed and screamed but the pain got worse and he kept trying to faint but he couldn't. When he eventually woke up he'd run the cold water in the sink in his room and hold his head under the tap . . .

There was the rapist again, staring at him. John said they had to use him like they'd used Barry for information. He reminded him of Barry, same yellow-tinted glasses, same gangly walk. He'd offer him a smoke.

Never seemed to have any visitors who brought him anything. Not like him. His girlfriend came regularly and brought him extra smokes. John said it wouldn't last. She'd get sick of it and get another bloke to look after her. Probably right. He knew about things and people. Specially people. Could pick a dirty a mile off. Said he could smell 'em in a crowded room. This dirty had raped girls, teenage girls. John said he'd been in here the longest. Said I had to talk to him, get his confidence. Hate it when John's angry with me. Hate it when he doesn't talk to me, when he treats me like I'm nothing. Like I'm just not there. Or like I'm stupid. He calls me Lurch. Couldn't survive being in here without him. Couldn't survive anywhere without him. He knows about the hurt. He knows it's like a festering toenail that spreads its poison until you cut it out, until you make the blood flow. He knows about the need to punish, how it makes you feel whole again, full again. The more of them you slice and dice the less of them there are to cause the hurt. They deserve it. You can never harm them enough, break them enough, burn them enough, beat them enough . . . nothing will ever be enough. Will it?

~

It's Sunday and there's a street festival called 'Hills On Hutt' where you can stroll along Hutt Street in the city, stopping at the stalls in front of all of the best restaurants and have matching wine and food fresh from the Adelaide Hills.

I'm standing on the Embassy balcony, looking north, remembering the traditional childhood Sunday afternoon drives with my parents and my grandfather to the cemetery at Golden Grove where my grandmother was buried. My schoolfriends thought it weird that we had picnics at the cemetery but they didn't know how much fun we all had there as a family. My four aunts and my mother would have baked on Saturday so that when we all arrived they could take out the folding picnic tables, cover them with freshly ironed tablecloths and spread them with scones and jam and cream and triple-layer sponges filled with cream and fresh strawberries. There'd be freshly baked cheese puffs and ham and mustard sandwiches. Thermoses of tea for the women, beer for the men and lemonade for the children. And then we would all troop across the road carrying fresh flowers and only when the grave was bursting with blooms were we allowed to run free, romping and whooping in the nearby open paddocks.

Golden Grove. Even the name denotes a kind of Hollywood heaven backlit by shafts of sunlight. I have the sudden urge to go there.

It's 2 pm and overcast but every now and again the sun breaks through and strengthens the purple blue intensity of the jacaranda trees. I drive through North Adelaide past the old-money mansions of Medindie, their lawns clipped and polished, their blinds drawn against the harsh antipodean light. Old

Adelaide money is still living inside some of these houses. Many of them are owned by widowed matrons whose housekeepers, imported from the old country, serve thin white cucumber sandwiches and slices of freshly baked fruit cake and cups of tea from the silver teapot, late in the afternoons inside shuttered rooms. I don't know any of these people and even if I did, they would never tell anyone their stories for public consumption. All their secrets will die with them. I've seen them at cocktail parties at Government House, their precious jewels hanging around shrivelled necks, sometimes on more formal occasions like the Queen's Birthday celebrations when long dresses are the order of the day, the almost transparent whiteness of the skin on their backs making them appear to be made of wax.

The early stretch of the Main North East Road is dominated on the left-hand side by the ugly 1960s building of the ABC, where once I sat behind a microphone and talked to the people of South Australia every morning. Even though I am travelling north, it seems to stay residential for a long time. I turn up Dvořák's New World Symphony on the radio. When I was young this was a new world of sorts, freshly minted suburbs. Finally, there appear the ubiquitous tawdry used car yards, Cash Converters, acres of petrol stations, trading posts. It's muggy now. Rain is hovering but patches of blue steal through the styrofoam-white clouds. The inside of the windscreen mists up.

When I was a child this was all paddocks with the odd lone horse flicking its tail against the flies. I think I've missed the turn and gone too far, but then I recognise the old stone church that used to stand in the middle of the dusty paddocks. It now has a sign on it saying 'Department of Family and Youth Services'. There could be a bulging file in there that has some of the murder victims' names in it. The department has never rung me to discuss my questions about child abuse in the area. Silly to think I'll just forget.

I turn left into Golden Grove Road. It's at least ten years since I've been here and then my Aunt Marjorie was driving, which was more of a worry than determining where we were going. How quickly nothing is familiar. It's all built up with beautifully neat, tiled-roof houses surrounded by gum trees and natural scrub. It's new but empty. Like Dry Creek. I don't think I ever remember seeing water in it.

Sunday, sleepy Sunday, yawning and lolling and idling by. I'm just continuing to drive in the hope that something will tell me I'm on the right road. Even though this is a two-lane freeway, I'm convinced they're the same gum trees that were always there. All gums look the same. Suddenly nothing is familiar. Absolutely nothing. I feel totally lost.

I come to an intersection, with a sign that says 'Yatala Vale Road', so Yatala prison must be a long way down the end of that road. No messages for me from their most infamous inmates. Silence is their creed.

There's a sign to the Tea Tree Players Theatre; no, I'm sure that's not right. I'm just going to stay on this road even though there're still houses. Hundreds of houses, they just sprang up like mushrooms after a good rain. On the right-hand side, though, there in the distance, is the quarry that I do remember. Finally I reach a roundabout and the sign says 'One Tree Hill, Golden Grove Cemetery'. I'm here. Now on my right, more huge quarries. Gaping cavities in a mouth full of teeth. And on my left, the Golden Grove Uniting Church. It had been the Presbyterian Church when my grandparents were married there. And there are the same ancient gum trees where Grandfather carved our names when we were children, when the sap was green and a heart shape was a promise of good things to come. And the same soft, rolling hills that we always thought, if we ran fast enough and far enough we were bound to reach the top, but never quite did before the echoes of our parents' voices called for us to come back.

It's now three o'clock in the afternoon. A cow moos softly in a far pasture. The small cemetery on my right is empty and totally silent. So, too, the church. Still and sweet with its natural stone and little porch with its red tin roof and rusty bell. The plaque says, 'June 24 AD MDCCCLXVI'. I'll have to work that out later. The hitching posts for the horses are still out the front. A faint memory of a visit with my grandfather, some kind of memorial service. He told me he had once hitched his horses to those posts. The original church has been extended but it's the same white picket fence.

The original cemetery is all plots and headstones, some of them extremely old. The newer addition on the left is lawn with small plaques and mounds of bright flowers. The old tap is still there. Walk up the main path, turn right and up the hill towards the oldest section with stone angels and rusted iron railings. And there it is – next door to Ivy White and Alan White, relatives of my grandmother, is the family plot. The worn gold lettering on a large salmon-pink marble headstone reads: 'In loving memory of Ethel Mary Woodhead, died October 16th, 1947, aged 65 years. Also John Frederick Wharton, beloved husband of above, died May 22nd, 1970, aged 87 years.'

My grandmother whom I never knew and my grandfather whom I adored. Whenever he stayed with us he'd clean my school shoes shiny bright; so, too, the coins tucked in the toes.

On a smaller headstone my parents: 'In loving memory of Sarah Jean Mitchell, died 23rd February, 1986, aged 75 years. Daughter of above, beloved wife of Irwin Mitchell, died 6th September, 1991, aged 86 years.'

'Hello, my darlings. It's Susan. I just want you to know that even though I don't visit here very often, not a day goes by when I don't think of you. You both loved me more than any child who ever lived.'

I pause, unused to such outbursts from my own lips.

A magpie caws and flies away, its wings beating hard against the still air. There goes my only audience.

I pick up the big empty vase, take it back to the rusty tap, fill it up with water as we had always done as children, carry it back to the grave and cram it with the yellow daisies I've brought with me.

'I'm writing a book about a couple of murderers. Well, it's not just about them. I know you would hate even the idea of it, Mum. Dad, you would just shake your head as if to say, "What next?" and then laugh. Grandfather, you would just say, "Come and sit on my knee and tell me the whole story." I'm so lucky to have had you as my family. You took such good care of me and surrounded me with such love that I took it all for granted. So many children never have that security or that stability, and they lead such sad and hopeless and twisted lives and . . .'

What was I doing, talking to headstones? Me, the perennial sceptic. Must be the sudden heat. I look up and squint. The sun is blasting out from behind the clouds. Hot pokers in my eyes. In my dreams it's always hot here, even though the borders of the cemetery are lined by the same Biblical palm trees. Definitely the same bothersome flies . . .

One day it will probably be my name on a plaque. Underneath my parents, inscribed here, fading and bleaching in the relentless sun.

I cross the road to inspect the largest gum tree. My grandfather always had his pocket knife with him and we would plead with him to carve our initials in the trunk. When we were children we thought they would remain there forever. Immortal, immovable. The trunk is bleached white and smooth under my fingers. Nearby, the grasses are golden. I pat the other khaki trees and finally the bare grey-white gum with the peeling brown bark. I say goodbye to the place where the picnic tables once stood and, strangely comforted, walk to the hire car without looking back.

One Tree Hill Road, faux Georgian mansions, the grand houses that people are building here now, cheek by jowl on such small blocks. Smaller families, larger homes. I decide on a whim to turn right into Yatala Vale Road, half-expecting to see a signpost to the jail. More new housing estates, this time with big signs announcing 'World's Best Address'. Tell that to Bunting and Wagner.

~

Yet another new housing estate. This time the road's called The Golden Way. Over the rise and there spread out before me are the squat flat plains of Adelaide. Red roofs on the horizon. Another new two-lane highway, which I know I've never been on before and have no idea where it's taking me, but I can see the city so I must be going in the right direction. There used to be endless fields of the purple weed called Salvation Jane; it choked everything else but was so pretty. They must have eradicated it. Or legislated against the colour purple.

I'm back to the six-lane highway that leads from Adelaide to Elizabeth. And, of course, on to the lush Barossa Valley. I turn left towards the city and the houses I'm now passing are much less grand, much smaller. Nevertheless, they've made an effort to maintain the natural bushland. Golden fields of dry grass. And then the looming dark-brown ruins of the Gepps Cross abattoir. Derelict now, all the windows broken, the building crumbling, only the animal sheds out the back still there. And the ghost of the young Bunting covered in blood. Red, sticky, clotted blood.

More blue sky. Enamelled. Oven blasts of heat. Eyeball-crushing light. Back through North Adelaide, crushed carpets of jacaranda blossoms, crimson gowns of full-flowering roses, swathes of green lawns, rows of bluestone villas and sandstone mansions.

Finally, the spires of St Peter's Cathedral, an institution under siege, an impending exposure of the enormous child sexual abuse among their clergy. Dark clouds of investigation.

Over the Torrens Bridge, its paddle-wheel boats called *Popeye* barely rippling the stagnant river. The Festival Centre and culture on the right, the parade grounds and the army on the left. The Women's Memorial Gardens, where they erect huge white marquees for Writers' Week. Government House and the monarchy opposite Parliament House and democracy. My eyes drift towards the plane trees now fully green, canopies lining the wide, planned, expansive streets.

I look up and nearly collide with a bus. Screech of brakes. Grip the wheel. Deep breath. Strange pulse in my right temple. The driver does not lean out of his window and swear at me or shake his fist. This is Adelaide, remember.

I note the destination of the bus. Its sign says Paradise (a suburb north east of the city). This is true. Cross my heart and hope to die.

I have nearly collided with Bus Number 174, the bus to Paradise.

That's what comes from visiting cemeteries and talking to headstones.

~

It was a long stretch until breakfast once they locked the doors to the straight row of cells in the high-security B Division of Yatala. The old familiar anger had knotted deep inside John Bunting . It sat like a live toad, squatting in his chest, ready, waiting to break through his skin. Just like the old days, the days before he discovered the cure. He sat on the edge of his narrow bed and rocked back and forth on his haunches. The rhythmic repetition helped him focus. He'd made a mistake with Vlassakis. Let the kid get under his guard. 'Will you be my father?' He had to admit, it had moved him, that plea. Done his best to teach him. Trained him. Talked to him. Tried to get him off the drugs. Kill you, those things. Mess with your head. Told him he had better things to do with his life, better ways to deal with the pain. Better ways to dissolve the anger. Thought he'd understood. He'd protected his mother too. But when her own mother died of cancer, she just gave up. On everything. Then she died of cancer too.

Taking the sickos to the clinic made him feel strong. Calmer. Like the cutting. The slicing and the dicing. He wanted to show them. Look, look at what I have done. Nothing to be in fear of, they're nothing but dead meat. He kept them in the barrels as a reminder. Rotting flesh. Exactly what they deserved. Putrid hunks of blood and bone. He should have dumped the barrels out at sea like he'd planned. He'd kept them as proof of his power. As proof that they were nothing. Nothing but a waste of space. He was ridding the world of its filth. Its waste.

But James had ruined it all. Year after year he'd beaten those dumb-arsed cops. Why? Because he was smart. He made plans. He gave orders. He lived off their money. Used their things. And those dirties got all they had coming. Every single one of them.

Miserable, filthy, stupid nothings. The slicing and the dicing calmed the squatting toad. The letting of blood, the screams, the burns, the pain. It all helped. But James was weak. He should have put him out of his misery like his brother, like all the other pieces of human shit he'd dispatched. He'd made them suffer first. They didn't die wondering. When he made them feel the pain, the toad was calm. But now it was back. Slimey, bug-eyed, ready to spring. The urgency was back too. The compulsion to plan, to think, to plot and finally to act. They thought they'd won by locking him away in here. Well, he'd show them. He was smarter than them. He'd beaten them before and he would do it again.

He wouldn't ever let anyone get to him like James again.

He'd fix him too. In time. No matter where he hid, he'd find him. He stopped rocking and got down on his knees. By sliding his hand carefully under the mattress on the bed he felt for the small secret pocket he had made inside the foam. Carefully, he lifted the flap and withdrew a small square of yellow Post-it notes. Turning on the television just in case one of the guards looked through the hatch, he began to slowly flip through the small yellow squares, many of which were covered in tiny writing, with headings in capitals underlined. Names and addresses and dates were numbered and neatly ordered. He picked up his right shoe and plunged his hand down towards the toe. When he withdrew it, he unwound a tight little ball of pink wool, slowly, carefully, in case it broke. One by one he placed the yellow squares of paper on the bed in order, and very carefully stretched the pink wool and linked it loosely from one small sheet to another. When the wool had run out, he stood back from the arrangement on the bed, placed his legs wide apart and stared at it. One by one he cracked his knuckles, first one hand and then the other.

And then he smiled.

~

In another cell, a few doors away, a large man with a T-shirt jammed in his mouth was writhing on his bed, eyes closed, his arms punching the air, his legs pummelling the mattress. There were tear-stains on his cheeks. The wet mouth of darkness swallowed his muffled cries.

~

On that same night in Delamere, a small village on the south coast, sat Christopher Pearson in a fraying cane chair on the front veranda of his large stone house. He loved to catch the last of the sunset before it disappeared, almost, it seemed, in the blink of an eye, below the horizon. He was alone with a bottle of French champagne. Most of his secret moments of joy had been experienced in silence. And in solitude. It didn't worry him that the tiles on the veranda were cracked, they reminded him of Rome. Nor did it worry him that the beautiful six-foot urn he had placed so carefully in the centre of the front garden was almost invisible because of the weeds, run rampant. These were suburban preoccupations that had no place in his world.

He was planning a major article of attack on the sunlit simplicities that passed for education in state schools. His head hummed with the power of withering words. His right foot tapped a tune. He poured himself another glass of champagne. Life was so full of possibilities, especially when you had an imagination seething with ideas. His mobile phone, on the table next to his glass, buzzed.

'What news from the Rialto, yes, hello . . .'

~

His neighbour in the city, Peter Goldsworthy, sat on his cast-iron balcony, looking out over one of Adelaide's major squares. He liked to share his pleasures and he'd poured a glass of crisp Sauvignon blanc for himself and his partner, Lisa, who was having a quick shower. He was planning an early night and would take the rest of the bottle into the bedroom. Like Martin, the character in his latest novel, a healthy cocktail of love and sex seemed to structure his days. He put these words in Martin's mouth: 'I often feel as if we are falling back towards bed all day, every day, from the moment we rise; returning, if obliquely, down some force-filled or gravitational gradient to our starting point, our separation each morning creating a latent energy that must be realised, made kinetic, sooner or later.'

Was Peter sick with the same bliss? Not just for Lisa but for this house where they lived, for the long walks around the city, for the drives through that earthly paradise called the Adelaide Hills, for the fresh food bought in the Central Market, for the wine tasted and bought straight from the wineries, for the hours of browsing through the art gallery and the museum and the library. This was the life he had secretly always dreamed of living ever since he was a small boy growing up in a fibro shack on the edge of a tiny country town where his father was a teacher of Latin.

He seemed alert to the thud of the water pipes signalling the end of her shower, as if he could smell her fresh skin. The darker side of his writing was nowhere in sight.

~

Two blocks away in an Italian restaurant called Chianti Classico, George Gross and Harry Watt were having dinner with a visiting designer from London who could not stop raving about the food and the wine and the weather. They had both heard the same responses many times before from visitors. The poor, deprived poms. They told him they were sorry, he couldn't stay at their beach house, a mere twenty-minute drive away at Henley Beach. In a surge of generosity they had lent it to some friends who were having their house renovated, and they hoped that their builder met his deadline because they really missed the beach. They could literally walk out of their front door across a small lawn onto the soft white sand and throw their bodies into the clear, cleansing waters of the ocean. Their London friend secretly planned to make another visit.

Not, they reassured him, that they didn't like having people to stay in their city apartment because they'd had some wonderful parties on the roof deck, especially at this time of the year. Only a few weeks ago they'd celebrated a friend's birthday up there but knowing that they had no room for a band as well as all the guests, they'd organised a crane to elevate the jazz band to play alongside the roof deck, where they danced happily all night by the light of the moon. Just like the Owl and the Pussycat.

Secretly, though, they couldn't wait to go home to the beach as summer was well and truly here. Harry longed to get a golden tan that lasted the whole season. As much as they loved Greece, Henley Beach was cleaner and closer and the souvlakis at Estia's restaurant on the seafront were just as good as those on the islands.

~

Penny Debelle and her young daughter had already finished dinner on the seafront at Henley Beach. Her husband was away and it was easier after a day of journalism for them to grab a meal at one of the cafés and go for a walk along the beach afterwards. The little waves splashed over their toes as they bent down to pick up shells for their collection at home. Penny was sure that she and her husband had been right to move back to Adelaide from Melbourne, where they had been working. They wanted their little girl – who had arrived much-wanted, late in their lives – to have the kind of childhood they had enjoyed growing up in Adelaide. They wanted her to know the ease and the delights of living in a house right on the beach and yet not having to spend hours travelling to school in the city. With the advent of email and the Internet, Penny could still write for the major papers in Melbourne and Sydney and live in Adelaide.

'One quick walk up the jetty and then home to bed.'

The crusty fishermen who spent every night throwing their lines and their crabnets over the side of the jetty smiled and waved at them.

'How are they biting?' she shouted.

'A bit slow. But the night is young.'

They said the same thing practically every night but always caught enough to keep themselves well fed.

She reminded herself she had to get up early in the morning to interview the lord mayor, who had just issued a special invitation for Prince Harry Windsor to spend some of his visit to Australia in Adelaide. He knew he was interested in Aboriginal paintings and thought that he might like to visit the South Australian Museum, which had the best Aboriginal collection in the southern hemisphere. She'd bet Harry would rather play polo.

~

Even though it was dark, Michael Harbison, Lord Mayor of Adelaide, was sitting under a white canvas umbrella outside one of his favourite cafés in the East End of Rundle Street having a quiet glass of red with Robert Champion de Crespigny, the Chancellor of the University of Adelaide and the man who had once owned the largest gold company in Australia. It was three times larger than the next biggest Australian gold company and the fifth-largest in the world. He had been born in Melbourne, made his fortune in Perth, had owned a house in the centre of Paris and had chosen to move his family to Adelaide in 1988. Having sold his latest acquisition, he had just given a year of his life without pay to help the premier get the new Economic Development Board up and running.

'I have given my time gladly. It really shouldn't be very hard to turn this state around almost overnight. That's the advantage of only a million people. We should use our smallness as a positive.'

Michael nodded his head. This was music to his ears. 'Don't take this the wrong way but sometimes I feel as if I can hold the entire city in the palm of my hand.'

Robert laughed and said: 'I understand the feeling. If there was a state in the world you'd want to take over, this is it. The word "unique" is so overused, but in the case of Adelaide, it's true.'

Michael shifted in his seat, not wanting to introduce a negative note, as the evening had been so positive. 'I understand that you upset people when you give speeches about their children having to go overseas to get experience.'

'I do. But I also tell the students to bring their experience back home so we can overcome this insularism. Some of the business community still don't understand that the reason we no longer have the main offices of Elders, SA Brewing, the Bank of Adelaide here any more is because they never included interstate directors on their boards and the world just passed them by. Problem is, they take criticism too personally.'

'What about all the Snowtown murder business?' asked Michael.

'We have to face our failures full-on and use them as an incentive to do better. No point in just pretending it didn't happen.'

'Do you really think Elizabeth will come good again?'

Robert looked him straight in the eyes and said: 'Yes, I do. And that's not just positive spin. Holden will expand enormously and there's also the defence industry. It will happen.'

Michael lifted his glass. 'Here's to Adelaide.'

Robert touched the side of Michael's glass lightly with his own. 'I genuinely love it, you know.'

~

At exactly that moment the Minister for Tourism, Jane Lomax-Smith, was sitting at a Tourism Awards Dinner in the Hyatt under a huge banner titled 'Secrets'. She raised her glass, toasting the film-maker Scott Hicks, who, having made it to the big time as a Hollywood director after the international success of his film *Shine*, had refused to leave Adelaide and move to a bigger city.

He leant across the table and said: 'If they want to see me in person, they have to come here. Why should I move? I have access to all of the things I need in a creative and technical sense and I'm an hour from the south coast that I adore.'

'Good for you,' she said.

One of the journalists also at the table, bored with the orgy of self-congratulation that inevitably accompanied such occasions, asked, 'Excuse me, Minister, but don't you think in the light of the Snowtown murders we ought to drop the word "Secrets" from our tourist promotions?'

All other conversation at the table ceased and she knew every eye was on her.

'On the contrary,' she said, well aware this would be quoted in the paper tomorrow. 'Just because a press lacking in imagination has to construct a weird and Gothic image for our city on the basis of a series of isolated murders, is no reason for us to over-react. I'm sure I don't have to repeat the real murder statistics to you. Adelaide is well known for being the nation's best-kept secret and tourists love to discover hidden delights. Take the negative and turn it into the positive, is my approach.'

'What about that woman in New South Wales, mother of four and an abattoir worker who stabbed her lover thirty-seven times and later cooked him and made soup with his head? If that had happened here you can imagine the furore. No-one called New South Wales the murder capital, even though it has lots more of those things happen than happen here,' said an earnest journalist from an opposing paper.

'Kangaroo soup, madam?' said the waitress to the minister.

'No, thank you. I think I'll pass tonight,' replied the minister, unable to stop herself bursting into hoots of laughter.

~

Across Victoria Square, next to the law courts, the premier was hosting a farewell dinner in the Hilton Hotel's prestigious Grange restaurant for his current British Thinker in Residence,

Charles Landry, an urban renewal and development expert. The premier was keen to know what he had decided about the city of Adelaide. Landry told him that he had undertaken a psychological profile of the city in much the same way you would a person. What had emerged most strongly was that the history of its foundation had shaped Adelaide's idea of itself and how it goes about its business. It has a preference for order and perfectionism, and Light's plan of the city was the supreme emblem of this. It has a sense of high-mindedness, a self-conception that is caring, ethical and reasonable, and a view that in the end it really is better than all those other upstart cities that have chosen to sacrifice good quality of life in order to chase gaudy ambitions. The premier sat quietly listening as Landry explained that within this settled order, creativity and radicalism are only occasionally allowed to burst out, as exemplified by the Dunstan era.

As if on cue, Cheong Liew, the restaurant's celebrated chef, appeared at the premier's side to ask if the food was up to standard. Cheong came to Adelaide as a migrant with an engineering degree. He started working in the kitchen at a restaurant called Neddy's and discovered his true passion was cooking. It was during the Dunstan era – Dunstan himself being an excellent cook and the author of a cookbook still in print – that Cheong experimented with what has now become the distinctive Australian style of cooking, the so-called 'fusion' between the European tradition and Asian herbs, spices and flavours. As the premier was explaining all this, Landry became very excited, clapped his hands and said: 'This is exactly what I am talking about. Fusion of ideas. You have to foster creativity on a continual basis, take considered risks, pick your niches carefully and push them tenaciously. Be bold. Go wild. Go outside the square. The challenge for Adelaide is not to be so defensive about itself. Just have the confidence to let the city's creativity

252

speak for itself. This food and this wine speak for themselves, you don't have to promote yourselves as "sensational Adelaide", simply being Adelaide is enough.' Everyone clapped, the premier nodded at the waiter and another bottle of Henschke's Hill of Grace was opened. In the time-honoured tradition of this city, a good thinker was a good drinker. And the city was, after all, as the premier assured him, like all things creative, a work in progress.

~

Also opening a second bottle of red wine that night, selecting it carefully from the cellar in his bluestone villa, was the man the city had dubbed the Prince of Darkness. Dr Perry was still more than a little shaken at the intensity of the vilification that had followed his interview. He could not understand why his fellow citizens had been so sensitive to his criticism. He meant well, he really did. How could he have touched a nerve that in all his previous hundreds of interviews he had never disturbed before? After all, he had only called it a 'stifled and inbred culture' and surely most people would agree with him about Elizabeth and similar areas of social deprivation. These killings were clearly linked to poverty, welfare dependency and the breakdown of family units. Perhaps he had not made a clear enough distinction between the city of Adelaide and its inner suburbs and these specific areas of impoverishment? Why did everyone want to believe that the city, all of it, every little bit of it, was perfect? What city was perfect? What human being was perfect?

This wine, however, was almost perfect. He must remember to order some more. The way he was going he'd be drinking most of it on his own, so many of his colleagues had refused invitations to dinner. Perhaps he would write an article about it. Force them to face up to the facts . . . What was that noise? Were they footsteps along the side of the house? Had he remembered to lock the back door? Now he was getting paranoid.

~

Pam Cleland had double-locked every door and window and checked them twice before she had gone to bed. She'd been forced to put on her glasses the second time because all that champagne had blurred her vision. She loved all those young people coming for drinks but it meant she had to focus on locking up properly after they'd all gone. That was the only thing wrong with living on your own in the middle of a tropical paradise. It could be a bit spooky at night. Oh well, she'd washed out her underclothes and tidied everything up just in case she died before morning. Settling into the luxury of her queen-size bed she turned up the evening concert on the bedside radio. Doubtless wouldn't be awake by the second movement but it was a lovely way to drift off. She could hear the gully breezes whipping their way through the forest of palms she had planted. Probably some old ghosts out there dancing naked in the moonlight. White bottoms flashing among the green fronds. So many parties, so much laughter, so many different people. Nureyev, Helpmann, Hepburn, Roma, John . . . all dead now. Death didn't scare her. She laughed out loud to herself. What fun they'd all had. What perfectly splendid fun.

~

Kym Bonython was sitting in his study. Having been forced to admit that his old motorbike was too big and heavy for him to handle, he had managed to sell it over the Internet, for a handsome profit to an English headmistress, of all people. Now he was conducting a secret search for another one, not so heavy. Everyone thought that because he was in his eighties he was going to give up his passion for riding them. Well, that was the wonderful thing about the Internet, you could buy and sell without anyone knowing. He turned up the volume of his original recording of Dave Brubeck's *Time Out* – it was still a brilliant piece of music, he must remember to play it on his radio program next week – and continued to search the World Wide Web. His next motorbike was just about at his fingertips.

~

On warm and pleasant nights like this, Robert Skewes liked to sit on his little front veranda in the moth-eaten armchair that had been his late mother's. Besides, it was too cluttered inside, what with all his collections and rubbish. Every day he tried to clear a space to sit but the stuff just kept spreading. This armchair was about the only comfortable place to sit. Just as well the warm weather had arrived.

'G'day, mate.' The voice startled him. 'Takin' the air, are ya?'

'Yeah,' said Skewes. He didn't know this bloke and he'd been a bit careful after what had happened with his last neighbours.

'Moved in just up the street. Bloody quiet, isn't it?'

'Yeah, that's how we like it.'

The man must have been in his thirties, medium height and build, cropped hair. He lit a cigarette and leant against the fence.

'How long you been here?' asked Skewes, making a small effort to be neighbourly.

'Only a couple a weeks, mate. Rent's cheap.'

'Won't find any cheaper.'

'They reckon this is the street where those Snowtown murderers lived. That right?'

'Yeah, that's right.'

'Did you know 'em?'

'I did, as a matter of fact.'

'Where exactly did they live?'

'Next door.'

'Is that right? Is that why there's no house?'

'They bulldozed it.'

'Should've made it a shrine, mate. Plenty of people would have come to have a look. You could've charged admission. They did the state a service getting rid of those perverts. More people oughtta do what they did. Too bad they got caught, mate, that's what I reckon. So do a lotta me mates. Can't trust the government to do away with 'em, can ya? Half of 'em are pooftas anyway. No, mate. Gotta take the law into your own hands. So, ya knew 'em did ya?'

'Yeah. They were my neighbours.'

He could have told him how they – Bunting, Lane and Wagner – had helped each other out with odd jobs, how Barry and Robert used to drive him to Salisbury in their car so he could do his shopping, go to the bank and get his disability pension. He could have told him how he had helped Bunting and Wagner fill in a hole under the rainwater tanks and then how, two years later, the police had dug up the remains of Suzanne Allen and Ray Davies from that same spot. He could have told him plenty. But he didn't.

'No sweat. I'll come round with a few beers tomorrow night and you can tell me all about it. Hey,' he leaned in closer towards Skewes in a conspiratorial manner, 'any more of those rock spiders living round here?'

Skewes stiffened in his chair. 'I wouldn't know.'

'Well, at least I know you're not one or ya wouldn't still be alive, would ya?'

When he laughed – more of a bark, really – at his own joke, Skewes thought the sound was familiar but couldn't quite place it. His memory wasn't as good as it used to be.

When he had finally finished laughing, the man coughed, spat and lit another cigarette, cupping his hand around the match. Skewes saw his face clearly in the light of the flame, only for a moment. It was just an ordinary face. Nothing to worry about.

~

By midnight most of the streets in the city of Adelaide were empty. The amber glow of the street lights barely lit up the pavements. Victoria Square was empty, too, except for the few stragglers who huddled around the Pie Cart, which served hot pies floating in bright green pea soup laced with tomato sauce that resembled a Dali painting. The Town Hall clock chimed the witching hour and Queen Victoria stood ramrod straight, no wind ruffling her bronze skirts. Adelaide slept. The hushed squares were breathing softly through the clipped green grass and the closed petals of the banked flowers. The good citizens were snuffling and snoring in their clean-sheeted suburban beds, the dogs twitching in their kennels and cats curled like furballs in their baskets, the children innocent in their dreams.

Evil was there too. Let's not pretend. One cannot exist without the other.

Every paradise has a snake or two slithering around, hidden beneath its lush exuberance. This is not the story of an evil city or even the story of evil men, it is the story of men who participated in evil and a city addicted to the notion of perfection.

Whatever that Utopian virus was that had caused the first settlers to leave their comfortable, middle-class homes and travel halfway across the world with all their precious belongings in order to create the best and the fairest society, it was still a virulent strain. Peter Goldsworthy was determined to write the quintessential Adelaide novel while leading his long-dreamt-of perfect life. Christopher Pearson gave the best years of his life to creating the perfect reflection of his adopted city back to itself in the *Adelaide Review*. Kym Bonython pined for it when he was away, and daily lived his passions with his fellow citizens. Pam Cleland just wanted it to be the place where everyone had the best possible fun. George Gross and Harry Who had sacrificed careers as international designers in order to have their ideal quality of life here. Jane Lomax-Smith had travelled from London to the Renaissance capital and, no longer content with being a doctor and a pathologist dealing with diseases of the body, now wants to heal the state. She wants it to be recognised as a beacon in a darkening world. She thinks that if we can't get it right in Adelaide, we can't get it right anywhere. The premier immigrated from working-class Britain to New Zealand to enter politics here because he fell under the spell of the charismatic Dunstan, who was determined to create the best and fairest and most sophisticated society in the southern hemisphere. The fire-eating lord mayor wants to turn it into a high-tech mini-Berlin and the founder of one of the world's largest gold companies has given a year of his life to help fulfil the premier's vision. Dr Perry, criminologist, arrived from New York to be part of the Dunstan experiment, instilled with the zeal to be part of a society where the urge was to change, to shape, to make possible the greatest good for the greatest number. In Adelaide, social idealism is not, and never has been, an impossible dream, it is the very stuff that dreams are made of.

The Nobel-prizewinning author J.M. Coetzee has recently moved from South Africa to settle here because, quite simply, he thinks 'it's heaven on earth'.

Even the murderer-vigilante, Bunting, came from Queensland and decided to stay in order to rid the city of what he believed were diseased paedophiles. He believed he had the cure to make the city a safe place for children. He did, however, allow this obsession to overtake him, with tragic consequences.

∼

I leant on my balcony in the still hush of this silken night and stared into the darkness. Out there, high on a nearby hill, pointing his finger at me, was Colonel William Light.

I pointed right back at him.

References

Linda Allery, *Elizabeth: From Dusty Plains to Royal Names: Oral Histories from the Elizabeth Community*, City of Elizabeth, 1996

Michael Burden, *Lost Adelaide: a photographic record*, Adelaide Booksellers, 2002

Stewart Cockburn, *Playford: Benevolent Despot*, Axiom, Kent Town, 1991

Geoffrey Dutton, *Founder of a City*, Cheshire, Melbourne, 1960

Peter Goldsworthy, *Three Dog Night*, Viking, Melbourne, 2003

Barbara Hanrahan, 'Weird Adelaide', the *Adelaide Review*, March 1988

Michael Jacobs, opinion piece, the *Adelaide Review*, October 2003

Susan Marsden, *Business, Charity and Sentiment*, Wakefield Press, South Australia, 1986

Mark Peel, *Good Times, Hard Times: The Past and the Future in Elizabeth*, Melbourne University Press, Melbourne, 1995

Douglas Pike, *Paradise of Dissent*, Melbourne University Press, Melbourne, 1957

Acknowledgements

My special thanks must go to the following:

Caroline MacFarlane and Maggie Tabberer, who first encouraged me to tackle this book; my agent Fiona Inglis, who championed it, and Tom Gilliatt of Pan Macmillan, who immediately and totally understood the purpose of my explorations.

All the people in Adelaide who openly or secretly spoke to me about the trial.

My cousins Chris, Lyn and Sarah John; my friends, Helen Norman, Garry Allan and Cate Fowler for help with research, and Sandy Lachlan for the loan of her house. Denise Von Wald provided me with all the information on festivals.

Special thanks to those who agreed to be interviewed for the book: Christopher Pearson, Peter Goldsworthy, Pam Cleland, Kym Bonython, George Gross and Harry Watt, The Hon Mike Rann, The Hon Jane Lomax-Smith, Lord Mayor of Adelaide Michael Harbison, Robert Champion de Crespigny, Dr Allan Perry, Russell Starkie, Michael Abbott, Q.C. Thank you to my trial companions for their generosity and help, in particular, Penny Debelle, Andrew McGarry and Marie McInerney.

Susie Carleton, Maggie Tabberer and Ingaborg and David

Caplice gave me shelter, food, wine and laughs when I most needed them. My accountant, John Eastwood, did his best to keep me on track. Nicholas and James Beasley constantly reminded me of the existence of innocence.

Sarina Rowell provided excellent feedback and editing, so too Karen Ward, and thank you to Nada Backovic for the wonderful cover.